Can-Do Attitude

Unlock Your True Potential and Achieve Unprecedented Success with the Power of a Can-Do Attitude: A Comprehensive Guide to Transform Your Mindset, Overcome Limiting Beliefs, and Cultivate the Mindset of Winners in All Areas of Life!

Lance P. Richards

I0625210

Can-Do Attitude: Unlock Your True Potential and Achieve Unprecedented Success with the Power of a Can-Do Attitude: A Comprehensive Guide to Transform Your Mindset, Overcome Limiting Beliefs, and Cultivate the Mindset of Winners in All Areas of Life!

Table of Contents

01: Introduction: The Power of a Can-Do Attitude

Do you ever feel like you're not living up to your true potential? Maybe you've tried to achieve certain goals in the past, but you always seem to fall short. Or perhaps you've convinced yourself that you're simply not capable of achieving greatness. Whatever the case may be, it's important to understand that your mindset plays a critical role in determining your level of success.

This is where the power of a can-do attitude comes in. A can-do attitude is a positive, optimistic, and proactive mindset that empowers you to take action towards your goals and overcome obstacles along the way. It's a mindset that says "I can" instead of "I can't," and it's the key to unlocking your true potential and achieving unprecedented success in all areas of your life.

In this comprehensive guide, we'll explore the power of a can-do attitude and provide you with the tools and strategies you need to cultivate this mindset in yourself. We'll start by examining the importance of mindset in determining your level of success and how limiting beliefs can hold you back from achieving your full potential. From there, we'll dive into the specific characteristics of a can-do attitude and show you how to adopt this mindset in your own life.

Along the way, we'll provide you with real-world examples of individuals who have achieved remarkable success through the power of a can-do attitude. From business leaders to athletes to everyday people, these individuals have all harnessed the power of a can-do attitude to overcome adversity and achieve their goals.

But before we dive into the specifics of cultivating a can-do attitude, let's first take a closer look at why mindset is so important when it comes to achieving success.

The Importance of Mindset

Your mindset is the lens through which you view the world. It's the set of beliefs and attitudes that shape your thoughts, feelings, and behaviors. And when it comes to achieving success, your mindset can be the determining factor in whether or not you reach your goals.

In fact, studies have shown that mindset can have a significant impact on your level of success. For example, research conducted by psychologist Carol Dweck found that individuals with a growth mindset – a belief that their abilities can be developed through hard work and dedication – were more likely to achieve success than those with a fixed mindset – a belief that their abilities are set in stone and cannot be changed.

This research highlights the fact that mindset can play a critical role in determining your level of success. If you believe that you're capable of achieving greatness and that your abilities can be developed through hard work and dedication, you're more likely to take action towards your goals and persist in the face of obstacles. On the other hand, if you believe that you're not capable of achieving greatness or that your abilities are fixed, you're more likely to give up when faced with challenges.

Limiting Beliefs

Unfortunately, many of us are held back by limiting beliefs – negative beliefs about ourselves, our abilities, and our potential. These limiting beliefs can be incredibly powerful, and they can prevent us from taking action towards our goals and achieving the success we desire.

For example, you might have a limiting belief that you're not smart enough to start your own business. As a result, you might never take the steps necessary to start your own company, even if you have a great idea and the necessary resources. Or you might have a limiting belief that you're not athletic enough to compete in a marathon. As a result, you might never train for a marathon or even attempt to run one.

The problem with limiting beliefs is that they're often based on false assumptions or outdated information. For example, you might believe that you're not smart enough to start your own business because you struggled in school with academic subjects. However, this belief ignores the fact that entrepreneurship requires a different set of skills than academic success, such as creativity, perseverance, and risk-taking.

Overcoming limiting beliefs requires a conscious effort to challenge and reframe these negative beliefs. This process involves questioning the evidence for these beliefs, seeking out counter-evidence, and replacing them with more posit-

ive and empowering beliefs. For example, if you have a limiting belief that you're not athletic enough to run a marathon, you might challenge this belief by seeking out stories
of individuals who started from scratch and trained their
way to completing a marathon. By doing so, you can reframe your belief from "I'm not athletic enough to run a
marathon" to "I can train and prepare myself to run a marathon if I'm willing to put in the effort."

Cultivating a Can-Do Attitude

Once you've challenged and reframed your limiting beliefs,
the next step is to cultivate a can-do attitude. A can-do attitude is a mindset that focuses on solutions rather than
problems, opportunities rather than limitations, and action
rather than inaction. Here are some key characteristics of a
can-do attitude:

Positive and Optimistic: A can-do attitude is characterized
by positivity and optimism. Rather than dwelling on negative thoughts or setbacks, individuals with a can-do attitude
focus on the positive aspects of a situation and look for opportunities to overcome challenges.

01: INTRODUCTION: THE POWER OF A CAN-DO ATTITUDE

Proactive and Resourceful: A can-do attitude is also marked by proactivity and resourcefulness. Rather than waiting for someone else to solve a problem or provide a solution, individuals with a can-do attitude take initiative and seek out resources and information to overcome obstacles.

Resilient and Persistent: A can-do attitude is also marked by resilience and persistence. Individuals with a can-do attitude understand that setbacks and failures are a natural part of the process and are willing to persist in the face of obstacles and challenges.

Growth-Oriented: Finally, a can-do attitude is growth-oriented, meaning that individuals with this mindset are focused on learning, growing, and developing their skills and abilities. Rather than seeing themselves as fixed or limited in their potential, individuals with a can-do attitude are open to feedback, willing to learn from their mistakes, and constantly seeking to improve themselves.

Putting It into Practice

Now that we've discussed the importance of mindset, the impact of limiting beliefs, and the key characteristics of a can-do attitude, let's talk about how to put this mindset into practice in your own life.

The first step is to become aware of your own mindset and the beliefs and attitudes that are holding you back. This requires a willingness to reflect honestly on your thoughts and behaviors and a commitment to challenging and reframing negative beliefs.

Next, it's important to focus on solutions rather than problems. When faced with a challenge or setback, ask yourself "What can I do to overcome this?" rather than "Why is this happening to me?" This shift in mindset can be incredibly powerful in empowering you to take action towards your goals.

It's also important to take proactive steps towards your goals. This might involve seeking out resources and information, taking courses or classes, networking with others in your field, or simply taking action towards your goals on a daily basis.

Finally, remember that setbacks and failures are a natural part of the process. Rather than letting these setbacks define you or your potential, focus on learning from them and using them as opportunities to grow and develop.

Conclusion

In conclusion, a can-do attitude is a powerful mindset that can unlock your true potential and enable you to achieve unprecedented success in all areas of your life. By cultivating a positive, proactive, and growth-oriented mindset, you can overcome limiting beliefs, focus on solutions rather than problems, and take proactive steps towards your goals.

02: What is a Can-Do Attitude?

Introduction

A can-do attitude is a mindset that empowers individuals to overcome challenges, embrace new opportunities, and achieve their goals. It is the belief that with hard work, perseverance, and a positive outlook, anything is possible. This chapter will explore what a can-do attitude is, why it is important, and how you can cultivate this mindset to achieve unprecedented success in all areas of your life.

Defining a Can-Do Attitude

A can-do attitude is a positive mindset that is characterized by optimism, resilience, and a willingness to take on challenges. It is the belief that with effort, hard work, and dedication, one can accomplish anything. A can-do attitude is not about denying the difficulties and obstacles that come with pursuing a goal, but rather it is about focusing on the opportunities and possibilities that exist.

Individuals with a can-do attitude approach challenges with a sense of curiosity and enthusiasm, rather than fear or apprehension. They view obstacles as opportunities to learn and grow, rather than as barriers to success. They are not discouraged by setbacks, but rather see them as temporary roadblocks that can be overcome with persistence and determination.

Why a Can-Do Attitude is Important

A can-do attitude is a critical component of success in all areas of life. Individuals who possess this mindset are more likely to achieve their goals, overcome obstacles, and reach their full potential. They are better equipped to handle stress, adapt to change, and bounce back from setbacks.

Moreover, a can-do attitude is contagious. It inspires others and creates a positive, supportive environment. People are drawn to those who exude positivity and optimism, and a can-do attitude can help foster strong relationships and networks.

Cultivating a Can-Do Attitude

While some people may naturally possess a can-do attitude, it is a mindset that can be cultivated and developed. The following strategies can help you adopt a can-do attitude and unleash your full potential.

02: WHAT IS A CAN-DO ATTITUDE?

Identify Limiting Beliefs

The first step in cultivating a can-do attitude is to identify and overcome limiting beliefs. These are beliefs that hold us back and prevent us from pursuing our goals. Limiting beliefs may include thoughts such as "I'm not smart enough," "I don't have the resources," or "I'm too old to start something new."

To overcome these limiting beliefs, it is essential to challenge them and replace them with empowering beliefs. For example, instead of thinking "I'm not smart enough," you might replace it with "I can learn anything if I put in the effort." By shifting your mindset in this way, you can open up new possibilities and opportunities.

Focus on Solutions, Not Problems

Individuals with a can-do attitude focus on solutions, not problems. When faced with a challenge, they do not dwell on the obstacles, but rather focus on finding a way to overcome them. They approach problems with a sense of curiosity and creativity, exploring different options until they find a solution.

02: WHAT IS A CAN-DO ATTITUDE?

To develop this mindset, it is important to reframe how you think about problems. Rather than viewing them as insurmountable obstacles, try to see them as opportunities to grow and learn. Adopt a solution-focused mindset, and you will be amazed at how much more effective and empowered you feel.

Take Action

A can-do attitude is all about taking action. Rather than waiting for things to happen, individuals with this mindset take proactive steps to achieve their goals. They are not afraid to take risks or make mistakes, recognizing that failure is a necessary part of the learning process.

To develop this mindset, it is important to take action, even if it is small. Start by setting small, achievable goals, and then take steps to accomplish them. As you begin to see progress, your confidence will grow, and you will be more motivated to take on bigger challenges.

Practice Gratitude

Gratitude is a powerful tool for cultivating a can-do attitude. By focusing on what we are grateful for, we can shift our mindset to one of abundance and positivity. Practicing gratitude can help us see the possibilities and opportunities that exist, rather than the obstacles and limitations.

To cultivate a sense of gratitude, take time each day to reflect on what you are thankful for. Write down three things you are grateful for each day, or simply take a few minutes to reflect on the blessings in your life. By practicing gratitude, you can develop a more positive outlook and a greater sense of optimism.

Surround Yourself with Positive People

The people we surround ourselves with have a significant impact on our mindset and outlook. To cultivate a can-do attitude, it is essential to surround yourself with positive, supportive people who encourage and inspire you.

Seek out individuals who share your goals and values, and who will support you in your journey. Avoid negative, toxic people who bring you down or discourage you from pursuing your dreams. By surrounding yourself with positivity and encouragement, you can cultivate a can-do attitude and unleash your full potential.

Conclusion

In conclusion, a can-do attitude is a powerful mindset that can help us achieve unprecedented success in all areas of life. It is a belief in our own ability to overcome obstacles, pursue our goals, and achieve our dreams. By identifying limiting beliefs, focusing on solutions, taking action, practicing gratitude, and surrounding ourselves with positive people, we can cultivate a can-do attitude and unlock our true potential. With this mindset, anything is possible, and we can achieve greatness in all areas of our lives.

03: The Science behind a Can-Do Attitude

Introduction:

A can-do attitude is an indispensable tool for success in every area of life, from personal to professional. It is the mindset that empowers individuals to tackle challenges with confidence and resilience, and to maintain a positive outlook despite setbacks and failures. A can-do attitude is what separates winners from losers, achievers from dreamers, and leaders from followers.

In this chapter, we will explore the science behind a can-do attitude, including the psychological and physiological mechanisms that underlie this mindset. We will examine the ways in which a can-do attitude can be developed and nurtured, and how it can be used to overcome limiting beliefs and achieve unprecedented success in all areas of life.

Section 1: The Psychology of a Can-Do Attitude

A can-do attitude is rooted in the psychology of optimism and resilience. Optimism is the belief that good things are more likely to happen than bad things, while resilience is the ability to bounce back from adversity. When combined, these two traits create a powerful psychological force that allows individuals to maintain a positive outlook, even in the face of adversity.

Research has shown that optimistic individuals are more likely to be successful in their careers, have better relation- ships, and experience better physical health than their pess- imistic counterparts. Optimistic individuals also tend to be more resilient, as they are better able to bounce back from setbacks and failures.

One of the key factors that contribute to a can-do attitude is self-efficacy, or the belief in one's ability to succeed. When individuals have high self-efficacy, they are more likely to take on challenging tasks, persist in the face of adversity, and ultimately achieve success. Self-efficacy is developed through a combination of experience, feedback, and social support.

Another important aspect of a can-do attitude is the ability to reframe negative situations in a positive light. This in- volves shifting one's perspective from a focus on the negat- ive aspects of a situation to a focus on the positive opportunities that can arise from it. This reframing process can help individuals to maintain a positive attitude, even in the face of adversity.

Section 2: The Physiology of a Can-Do Attitude

The physiological mechanisms that underlie a can-do attitude are complex and multifaceted. At a basic level, a can-do attitude is associated with the release of neurotransmitters such as dopamine, serotonin, and endorphins, which are involved in feelings of pleasure, reward, and well-being.

Studies have also shown that a can-do attitude is associated with lower levels of stress hormones such as cortisol and adrenaline. When individuals have a can-do attitude, they are better able to regulate their stress response and maintain a sense of calm and control, even in challenging situations.

In addition to these hormonal responses, a can-do attitude is also associated with changes in brain activity. When individuals approach tasks with a can-do attitude, there is increased activity in the prefrontal cortex, which is involved in planning, decision-making, and goal-setting. This increased activity in the prefrontal cortex is thought to facilitate problem-solving and creative thinking, allowing individuals to overcome obstacles and achieve success.

Section 3: Developing a Can-Do Attitude

While some individuals may be naturally predisposed to a can-do attitude, it is also a mindset that can be developed and nurtured over time. The following strategies can help individuals to cultivate a can-do attitude:

Focus on strengths: By identifying and focusing on their strengths, individuals can build confidence and self-efficacy, which are key components of a can-do attitude.

Set achievable goals: By setting small, achievable goals, individuals can build momentum and develop a sense of accomplishment, which can fuel a can-do attitude.

Embrace failure: Rather than viewing failure as a negative outcome, individuals with a can-do attitude view failure as an opportunity to learn and grow. By reframing failure in this way, individuals can develop resilience and perseverance.

Practice positivity: By intentionally focusing on positive aspects of life and situations, individuals can train their brains to see opportunities instead of obstacles. This practice can help to develop a can-do attitude over time.

Surround oneself with positivity: By surrounding oneself with positive and supportive people, individuals can develop a sense of community and social support, which can help to build a can-do attitude.

Practice self-care: By prioritizing self-care activities such as exercise, healthy eating, and getting enough sleep, individuals can promote physical and mental health, which is essential for developing and maintaining a can-do attitude.

Practice mindfulness: By practicing mindfulness techniques such as meditation, individuals can develop greater awareness and control over their thoughts and emotions, which can help to promote a can-do attitude.

Conclusion:

A can-do attitude is a powerful mindset that can help individuals to achieve unprecedented success in all areas of life. By understanding the psychology and physiology that underlie this mindset, and by cultivating the strategies outlined above, individuals can develop and nurture a can-do attitude that will serve them well in all aspects of their lives. With a can-do attitude, anything is possible!

04: The Benefits of a Can-Do Attitude

Introduction

Have you ever wondered what separates the most successful people in the world from the rest? Is it their intelligence, talent, or resources? While these factors do play a role in one's success, the most critical factor is their mindset. People who achieve unprecedented success possess a can-do attitude, a mindset that allows them to overcome obstacles, take risks, and pursue their goals with unwavering determination. In this chapter, we will discuss the benefits of cultivating a can-do attitude and how it can transform your life.

Boost Your Confidence

One of the most significant benefits of a can-do attitude is that it boosts your confidence. When you believe that you can accomplish anything you set your mind to, you develop an unwavering self-confidence that propels you forward. Confidence is crucial in all areas of life, from personal relationships to career success. People with confidence are more likely to take risks, seize opportunities, and bounce back from setbacks. When you believe in yourself, others will believe in you too.

Overcome Limiting Beliefs

Another benefit of a can-do attitude is that it helps you overcome limiting beliefs. Limiting beliefs are negative thoughts that hold you back from reaching your full potential. These beliefs are often ingrained in us from childhood and can be challenging to overcome. However, when you adopt a can-do attitude, you learn to challenge these beliefs and replace them with positive, empowering thoughts. With practice, you can retrain your brain to focus on possibilities rather than limitations.

Increase Resilience

Resilience is the ability to bounce back from setbacks and overcome adversity. When you have a can-do attitude, you develop a strong sense of resilience. You understand that failure is not a reflection of your worth or abilities, but rather a necessary part of the learning process. People with resilience are better equipped to handle life's challenges and come out stronger on the other side. With a can-do attitude, you develop the resilience to face any obstacle and overcome it with grace and determination.

Develop a Growth Mindset

A growth mindset is a belief that one's abilities can be developed through dedication and hard work. People with a growth mindset understand that intelligence and talent are not fixed traits but can be improved with effort. A can-do attitude is the foundation of a growth mindset. When you believe that you can achieve anything with hard work and determination, you develop a mindset that is open to learning and growth. With a growth mindset, you are more likely to embrace challenges, seek out new opportunities, and push yourself out of your comfort zone.

Improve Relationships

Having a can-do attitude can also improve your relationships. When you believe in yourself and your abilities, you are more likely to form positive relationships with others. People are naturally drawn to those who exude confidence and positivity. With a can-do attitude, you are more likely to form healthy relationships that are based on mutual respect, trust, and support. When you have strong relationships, you have a support system that can help you through tough times and celebrate your successes.

Increase Productivity

Finally, a can-do attitude can increase your productivity. When you believe that you can accomplish anything you set your mind to, you are more likely to take action and get things done. You have a sense of urgency and focus that propels you forward. With a can-do attitude, you are less likely to procrastinate or make excuses. You understand that every moment counts and that you must make the most of your time to achieve your goals.

Conclusion

In conclusion, a can-do attitude is a mindset that can transform your life in countless ways. It can boost your confidence, help you overcome limiting beliefs, increase your resilience, develop a growth mindset, improve your relationships, and increase your productivity. Cultivating a can-do attitude is not easy, but with practice and effort, it is possible. Start by challenging your negative thoughts and replacing them with positive ones. Set realistic goals and take small steps towards achieving them. Surround yourself with people who believe in you and support your goals. Celebrate your successes, no matter how small they may be. Remember that every setback is an opportunity to learn and grow. With a can-do attitude, you can unlock your true potential and achieve unprecedented success in all areas of your life.

However, it's important to note that having a can-do attitude does not mean that you should ignore your limitations or take unnecessary risks. It's essential to be realistic and evaluate your abilities and resources before taking action. While a can-do attitude can help you overcome obstacles, it's important to have a backup plan in case things don't go as planned.

Furthermore, cultivating a can-do attitude requires ongoing effort and practice. It's easy to slip back into negative thought patterns, especially during difficult times. That's why it's essential to make a conscious effort to maintain a positive mindset and surround yourself with people who support your goals. You can also engage in activities that boost your confidence and sense of achievement, such as exercise, learning new skills, or volunteering.

In conclusion, a can-do attitude is a powerful tool that can help you overcome obstacles, achieve your goals, and live a fulfilling life. It's a mindset that is rooted in positivity, resilience, and self-belief. While cultivating a can-do attitude requires effort and practice, the benefits are well worth it. With a can-do attitude, you can unlock your true potential and achieve unprecedented success in all areas of your life.

05: Overcoming Negative Self-Talk and Limiting Beliefs

Introduction:

The way we talk to ourselves has a profound impact on our lives. Negative self-talk and limiting beliefs can hold us back from achieving our full potential and living the life we truly desire. They can sabotage our efforts and create self-doubt, fear, and anxiety, preventing us from taking action towards our goals.

In this chapter, we will explore how to identify negative self-talk and limiting beliefs, understand how they affect us, and most importantly, learn how to overcome them with the power of a can-do attitude. We will provide you with practical strategies to transform your mindset, boost your confidence, and cultivate the mindset of winners in all areas of life.

Identifying Negative Self-Talk:

Negative self-talk is the inner voice that we all have, which tells us what we can and cannot do. It is the voice that criticizes us, doubts our abilities, and tells us that we are not good enough. Negative self-talk can take many forms, such as "I'm not smart enough," "I'll never be able to do it," or "I always mess things up."

To overcome negative self-talk, we first need to identify it. Pay attention to the words you use when you talk to yourself. Notice if you tend to use negative words or phrases, such as "never," "can't," or "won't." Also, be aware of the tone of your inner voice. Does it sound critical, judgmental, or harsh?

Understanding Limiting Beliefs:

Limiting beliefs are the beliefs we hold about ourselves and the world that restrict us from achieving our full potential. They are often rooted in past experiences, traumas, or societal conditioning. Limiting beliefs can take many forms, such as "I'm not good enough," "Money is hard to come by," or "Success is only for the lucky ones."

To overcome limiting beliefs, we need to understand them. Ask yourself what beliefs you hold about yourself and the world. Are they empowering or limiting? Where do these beliefs come from? Are they based on facts or assumptions?

05: OVERCOMING NEGATIVE SELF-TALK AND LIMITING BELIEFS

Once you have identified your limiting beliefs, you can start to challenge them.

Challenging Negative Self-Talk and Limiting Beliefs:

Now that you have identified your negative self-talk and limiting beliefs, it's time to challenge them. One effective way to do this is to question their validity. Ask yourself if they are based on facts or assumptions. For example, if you believe that you are not good enough, ask yourself what evidence you have to support this belief. Is it based on past failures or rejections? If so, remind yourself that failure is a natural part of the learning process, and it does not define your worth or potential.

Another way to challenge negative self-talk and limiting beliefs is to reframe them. Reframing means looking at a situation from a different perspective. For example, instead of saying, "I can't do it," reframe it as, "I haven't figured it out yet." This shift in perspective can help you see the situation as a challenge rather than a roadblock, and it can give you the motivation to keep trying.

Developing a Can-Do Attitude:

05: OVERCOMING NEGATIVE SELF-TALK AND LIMIT-ING BELIEFS

To cultivate a can-do attitude, we need to focus on our strengths and abilities. We need to shift our mindset from one of self-doubt to one of self-belief. One effective way to do this is to create a list of our accomplishments, strengths, and positive qualities. Remind yourself of all the times you have succeeded and all the things you are good at. Use this list as a reminder of your potential and capabilities.

Another way to develop a can-do attitude is to set achievable goals. Start small and work your way up. Celebrate your successes, no matter how small they may seem, and use them as motivation to keep going. As you achieve each goal, set a new one, gradually increasing the level of difficulty. This will help build your confidence and reinforce the belief that you can accomplish anything you set your mind to.

Finally, surround yourself with positive and supportive people. Seek out mentors, coaches, or friends who believe in you and your abilities. Avoid negative people who bring you down or reinforce your negative self-talk and limiting beliefs. Remember, you are the average of the five people you spend the most time with, so choose wisely.

05: OVERCOMING NEGATIVE SELF-TALK AND LIMITING BELIEFS

Conclusion:

Overcoming negative self-talk and limiting beliefs is a crucial step towards developing a can-do attitude and achieving unprecedented success in all areas of life. By identifying our negative self-talk and limiting beliefs, challenging them, and developing a positive mindset, we can unlock our true potential and live the life we truly desire.

Remember, your thoughts create your reality. Choose your thoughts wisely, and always believe in yourself. With a can-do attitude, anything is possible.

06: The Connection between Mindset and Success

The mindset that we have can have a profound impact on our success in life. It is the way that we think, the beliefs that we hold, and the attitudes that we adopt that ultimately shape our actions and our outcomes. In this chapter, we will explore the connection between mindset and success, and the ways in which we can cultivate a can-do attitude to unlock our true potential and achieve unprecedented success in all areas of our lives.

The Power of Mindset

At its core, mindset is a set of beliefs and attitudes that shape our thoughts and actions. It is the lens through which we view the world and the filter through which we interpret our experiences. Research has shown that mindset has a significant impact on our performance, our resilience, and our ability to achieve our goals.

For example, people with a growth mindset, who believe that their abilities can be developed through hard work and dedication, are more likely to embrace challenges, persist in the face of setbacks, and ultimately achieve greater success than those with a fixed mindset, who believe that their abilities are set in stone and cannot be changed.

Similarly, people who have a can-do attitude, who believe that they are capable of overcoming obstacles and achieving their goals, are more likely to take risks, seize opportunities, and ultimately achieve their desired outcomes than those who have a defeatist attitude, who believe that they are powerless to change their circumstances and are doomed to failure.

The Impact of Limiting Beliefs

Unfortunately, many of us hold limiting beliefs that can hold us back from achieving our full potential. These beliefs may be rooted in past experiences, societal messages, or even our own negative self-talk. Examples of limiting beliefs include "I'm not smart enough," "I'll never be successful," or "I'm not worthy of love and respect."

When we hold onto these limiting beliefs, they can become self-fulfilling prophecies, shaping our actions and ultimately leading to outcomes that confirm our negative beliefs. For example, if we believe that we are not smart enough, we may avoid challenges that could help us grow and learn, ultimately limiting our opportunities for success.

The good news is that we can learn to overcome our limiting beliefs and cultivate a more positive mindset. By adopting a can-do attitude and embracing a growth mindset, we can develop the resilience and determination that we need to overcome obstacles and achieve our goals.

How to Cultivate a Can-Do Attitude

So, how can we cultivate a can-do attitude and overcome our limiting beliefs? Here are some tips:

Practice positive self-talk: The way that we talk to ourselves can have a powerful impact on our mindset. Try to replace negative self-talk with positive affirmations. For example, instead of saying "I can't do this," try saying "I can do this with practice and effort."

Embrace challenges: Instead of avoiding challenges, try to embrace them as opportunities for growth and learning. Recognize that setbacks and failures are a natural part of the learning process, and that they can help you build resilience

34

and develop new skills.

Celebrate your successes: When you achieve a goal, take the time to celebrate your success. Recognize the hard work and effort that went into achieving your goal, and use that sense of accomplishment to fuel your motivation for future success.

Surround yourself with positive influences: Seek out supportive friends and mentors who can provide encouragement and inspiration. Read books and listen to podcasts that promote a can-do attitude and a growth mindset.

Practice gratitude: Gratitude can help shift our focus away from negative thoughts and towards the positive aspects of our lives. Take time each day to reflect on the things that you are grateful for, and use that gratitude to cultivate a positive mindset.

By adopting a can-do attitude and embracing a growth mindset, we can begin to reframe our thoughts and beliefs in a more positive light. We can begin to see challenges as opportunities, failures as learning experiences, and setbacks as temporary roadblocks on the path to success.

06: THE CONNECTION BETWEEN MINDSET AND SUC-CESS

It's important to note that cultivating a can-do attitude is not something that happens overnight. It takes time, effort, and a willingness to challenge our own beliefs and assumptions about ourselves and the world around us. However, the rewards of developing a positive mindset are immeasurable. By cultivating a can-do attitude, we can unlock our true potential and achieve unprecedented success in all areas of our lives.

The Role of Mindset in Success

The connection between mindset and success is well-documented. Studies have shown that people with a growth mindset are more likely to achieve their goals and perform at a higher level than those with a fixed mindset. Additionally, individuals who adopt a can-do attitude and embrace a growth mindset are more likely to persist in the face of obstacles, take calculated risks, and ultimately achieve greater success than those with a defeatist attitude.

One of the key ways in which mindset impacts success is through our ability to manage stress and overcome setbacks. When we have a positive mindset, we are better equipped to cope with the challenges and setbacks that inevitably arise on the path to success. We are able to bounce back from failures, learn from our mistakes, and keep moving forward towards our goals.

In addition, a positive mindset can help us cultivate the resilience and determination that we need to overcome obstacles and achieve our goals. When we believe in ourselves and our abilities, we are more likely to take action towards our goals, even in the face of uncertainty or adversity.

Ultimately, the connection between mindset and success is a powerful one. By cultivating a can-do attitude and embracing a growth mindset, we can unlock our true potential and achieve unprecedented success in all areas of our lives.

Conclusion

In conclusion, mindset plays a crucial role in our ability to achieve success in life. By adopting a can-do attitude and embracing a growth mindset, we can reframe our thoughts and beliefs in a more positive light, overcome our limiting beliefs, and ultimately achieve our goals. While cultivating a positive mindset takes time and effort, the rewards are immeasurable. By embracing a can-do attitude, we can unlock our true potential and achieve unprecedented success in all areas of our lives.

07: The Importance of Setting Goals with a Can-Do Attitude

Introduction

A can-do attitude is essential to achieving success in any area of life. It is the mindset that enables individuals to believe in their ability to overcome obstacles and accomplish their goals. One of the crucial aspects of a can-do attitude is goal setting. In this chapter, we will discuss the importance of setting goals with a can-do attitude, how to set effective goals, and the benefits of achieving those goals.

The Importance of Setting Goals

Setting goals is essential because it provides individuals with direction and focus. Without goals, we tend to drift through life, reacting to whatever comes our way. By setting goals, we are taking control of our lives and creating a roadmap to follow. Goals give us a purpose and a reason to wake up every morning.

Goals also provide motivation. When we have a specific target to aim for, we are more likely to stay focused and committed. Goals give us something to work towards, and the satisfaction of achieving those goals is a powerful motivator. It is important to note that the more significant the goal, the more motivation it can provide.

Setting goals with a can-do attitude is even more important. A can-do attitude means believing that anything is possible with the right mindset and effort. By setting goals with this mindset, we are more likely to achieve them. We are not deterred by obstacles or setbacks because we know that we have the ability to overcome them.

How to Set Effective Goals

Setting effective goals requires more than just writing down a list of things we want to accomplish. It requires a strategic approach that takes into account our values, priorities, and resources. Here are some steps to help set effective goals:

Step 1: Identify What You Want

The first step in setting goals is to identify what you want to achieve. This can be a specific outcome, such as running a marathon, or a general goal, such as improving your health.

Step 2: Make Your Goals SMART

07: THE IMPORTANCE OF SETTING GOALS WITH A CAN-DO ATTITUDE

Once you have identified what you want to achieve, it's essential to make your goals SMART:

– Specific: Clearly define what you want to accomplish.

– Measurable: Create a way to measure progress towards your goal.

– Achievable: Make sure your goal is attainable given your resources and skills.

– Relevant: Ensure your goal is relevant to your values and priorities.

– Time-bound: Set a deadline for achieving your goal.

By making your goals SMART, you will be more likely to achieve them because they are well-defined and achievable.

Step 3: Break Down Your Goals

Breaking down your goals into smaller, more manageable steps can make them seem less daunting. It also provides a roadmap to follow, making it easier to stay focused and motivated.

07: THE IMPORTANCE OF SETTING GOALS WITH A CAN-DO ATTITUDE

Step 4: Create a Plan of Action

Creating a plan of action that outlines what you need to do to achieve your goals is essential. This can include setting milestones, creating a schedule, and identifying resources you may need.

Benefits of Achieving Your Goals

Achieving your goals has many benefits. Here are a few:

– Sense of Accomplishment: Achieving your goals provides a sense of accomplishment and boosts self-esteem.

– Increased Motivation: Accomplishing one goal can provide the motivation to tackle more challenging goals.

– Improved Self-Discipline: Setting and achieving goals requires self-discipline, which can improve other areas of life.

– Clearer Direction: Achieving goals provides a clearer direction and focus, making it easier to navigate life's challenges.

– Expanded Comfort Zone: Accomplishing goals often requires stepping outside of our comfort zones, which can lead to personal growth and development.

Conclusion

Setting goals with a can-do attitude is essential to achieving success in any area of life. Goals provide direction, motivation, and a sense of purpose. By making your goals SMART, breaking them down into manageable steps, and creating a plan of action, you can increase your chances of achieving them. The benefits of achieving your goals are numerous, including a sense of accomplishment, increased motivation, and improved self-discipline.

It's important to remember that setting goals is not a one-time event. As we grow and evolve, our goals may change. It's essential to review and adjust our goals periodically to ensure they are still relevant and aligned with our values and priorities.

In addition to setting goals, it's also crucial to adopt a can-do attitude. A can-do attitude means believing in yourself and your abilities, even in the face of challenges or setbacks. It means approaching obstacles with a positive and proactive mindset, looking for solutions rather than dwelling on the problem.

When we combine a can-do attitude with effective goal setting, we unlock our true potential and achieve unprecedented success in all areas of life. We become unstoppable, empowered to create the life we desire.

In conclusion, setting goals with a can-do attitude is an essential aspect of achieving success in life. By following the steps outlined in this chapter and adopting a positive and proactive mindset, you can set and achieve goals that will transform your life. So go ahead, set those goals, believe in yourself, and unleash your true potential!

08: Developing a Can-Do Attitude in Your Personal Life

Introduction

Your attitude is one of the most powerful tools you have at your disposal. It can either propel you towards success or hinder your progress. A can-do attitude is essential to achieve unprecedented success in all areas of life. It's a mindset that enables you to face challenges, overcome obstacles, and keep moving forward. In this chapter, we'll explore how you can develop a can-do attitude in your personal life and reap the benefits of this powerful mindset.

Identify Your Limiting Beliefs

The first step in developing a can-do attitude is to identify your limiting beliefs. These are the beliefs that hold you back and prevent you from achieving your goals. Limiting beliefs can manifest in many forms, such as fear of failure, self-doubt, or the belief that you're not good enough. Once you identify your limiting beliefs, you can work on replacing them with empowering beliefs that support your success.

Reframe Your Mindset

08: DEVELOPING A CAN-DO ATTITUDE IN YOUR PERSONAL LIFE

Reframing your mindset is a powerful way to develop a can-do attitude. It involves looking at situations in a new light and focusing on the positive aspects rather than the negative ones. For example, instead of focusing on the challenges you may face when pursuing a new goal, focus on the benefits you'll receive once you achieve it. Reframing your mindset can help you stay motivated and focused on your goals.

Set Realistic Goals

Setting realistic goals is an essential part of developing a can-do attitude. When you set goals that are achievable, you'll be more likely to accomplish them, which will give you a sense of accomplishment and confidence. Start by setting small goals that are within your reach and gradually work your way up to more challenging ones. Celebrate each accomplishment, no matter how small, as it will help you build momentum and confidence.

Embrace Failure as a Learning Opportunity

Failure is an inevitable part of life, and learning how to embrace it as a learning opportunity is essential to developing a can-do attitude. When you fail, take the time to reflect on what went wrong, what you could have done differently, and what you learned from the experience. Use this knowledge to adjust your approach and try again. Remember, failure is not the end; it's an opportunity to grow and learn.

Practice Gratitude

Practicing gratitude is a powerful way to cultivate a can-do attitude. It involves focusing on the positive aspects of your life and expressing gratitude for them. When you focus on the good things in your life, you'll be more likely to have a positive outlook on life, which will help you develop a can-do attitude. Take the time each day to express gratitude for the people, experiences, and things in your life that bring you joy.

Surround Yourself with Positive People

Surrounding yourself with positive people is essential to developing a can-do attitude. When you're around people who support and encourage you, you'll be more likely to adopt their mindset and beliefs. Seek out people who inspire you, encourage you, and challenge you to be your best self. These people will help you stay motivated and focused on your goals.

Take Action

Taking action is the most critical part of developing a can-do attitude. It's not enough to have a positive mindset; you must also take action towards your goals. Start by taking small steps each day that will bring you closer to your goals. These small steps will add up over time and help you achieve your goals. Remember, the key to success is consistent, focused action.

Conclusion

Developing a can-do attitude in your personal life is essential to achieve unprecedented success in all areas of life. It's a mindset that enables you to face challenges, overcome obstacles, and keep moving forward. By identifying your limiting beliefs, reframing your mindset, setting realistic goals, embracing failure as a learning opportunity, practicing gratitude, surrounding yourself with positive people, and taking action, you can cultivate a can-do attitude that will help you achieve your wildest dreams.

08: DEVELOPING A CAN-DO ATTITUDE IN YOUR PER-SONAL LIFE

It's important to remember that developing a can-do attitude is not something that happens overnight. It takes time, effort, and consistent practice. But with dedication and commitment, you can transform your mindset and achieve unprecedented success in all areas of life.

As you work towards developing a can-do attitude, it's important to be kind and patient with yourself. Celebrate your successes, no matter how small, and learn from your failures. Remember, success is not about being perfect; it's about progress and growth.

In conclusion, developing a can-do attitude in your personal life is a powerful way to unlock your true potential and achieve unprecedented success in all areas of life. By identifying your limiting beliefs, reframing your mindset, setting realistic goals, embracing failure as a learning opportunity, practicing gratitude, surrounding yourself with positive people, and taking action, you can cultivate a mindset of winners that will help you achieve your wildest dreams. So start today, take the first step towards developing a can-do attitude, and watch as your life transforms before your very eyes.

09: Developing a Can-Do Attitude in Your Professional Life

In today's highly competitive world, having a can-do attitude is not only desirable but necessary to succeed in your professional life. It is a mindset that empowers you to overcome challenges, take calculated risks, and seize opportunities that others might miss. It is the difference between someone who achieves great things and someone who settles for mediocrity. In this chapter, we will explore the steps you can take to develop a can-do attitude in your professional life and unlock your true potential.

Identify Your Limiting Beliefs

The first step in developing a can-do attitude is to identify your limiting beliefs. These are the thoughts and beliefs that hold you back from pursuing your goals and achieving your full potential. They are the stories you tell yourself about why you can't do something or why you're not good enough. Once you identify your limiting beliefs, you can begin to challenge them and replace them with more empowering beliefs.

Embrace a Growth Mindset

09: DEVELOPING A CAN-DO ATTITUDE IN YOUR PRO-FESSIONAL LIFE

The second step is to embrace a growth mindset. This is the belief that your abilities and intelligence can be developed through hard work, dedication, and a willingness to learn. People with a growth mindset see challenges as opportunities to learn and grow, while those with a fixed mindset see challenges as obstacles that cannot be overcome. By embracing a growth mindset, you will be more open to new experiences, more resilient in the face of setbacks, and more willing to take on challenges.

Set Clear Goals

The third step is to set clear goals. People with a can-do attitude have a clear vision of what they want to achieve, and they take concrete steps to make it happen. Setting clear goals helps you focus your energy and attention on what matters most, and it gives you a sense of purpose and direction. When setting goals, make sure they are specific, measurable, achievable, relevant, and time-bound.

Take Action

The fourth step is to take action. A can-do attitude is not just about thinking positive thoughts; it's about taking concrete steps to achieve your goals. This means stepping out of your comfort zone, taking risks, and embracing uncertainty. When you take action, you build momentum, and you create a sense of accomplishment that fuels your motivation and drive.

Cultivate Resilience

The fifth step is to cultivate resilience. Resilience is the ability to bounce back from setbacks and overcome challenges. People with a can-do attitude are resilient because they see setbacks as temporary and are willing to try again. Cultivating resilience requires developing a growth mindset, building a support network, and practicing self-care.

Celebrate Your Successes

The sixth step is to celebrate your successes. People with a can-do attitude take time to acknowledge and celebrate their achievements, no matter how small. Celebrating your successes helps you build confidence, reinforce positive habits, and stay motivated. It also helps you appreciate the journey and enjoy the process of achieving your goals.

09: DEVELOPING A CAN-DO ATTITUDE IN YOUR PRO-FESSIONAL LIFE

Learn from Failure

The seventh step is to learn from failure. Failure is an inevitable part of any journey, and people with a can-do attitude use it as an opportunity to learn and grow. When you experience failure, take the time to reflect on what went wrong and what you can do differently next time. Use failure as a stepping stone to success, not a barrier to your progress.

In conclusion, developing a can-do attitude in your professional life is essential if you want to achieve unprecedented success. It requires identifying your limiting beliefs, embracing a growth mindset, setting clear goals, taking action, cultivating resilience, celebrating your successes, and learning from failure. By following these steps, you can unlock your true potential, overcome obstacles, and cultivate the mindset of winners in all areas of life. Remember, anything is possible with a can-do attitude!

10: Cultivating Resilience and Persistence with a Can-Do Attitude

In life, we all face challenges, setbacks, and obstacles. Some of these challenges can be small, while others can be significant and life-changing. The way we handle these challenges can have a significant impact on our lives and our ability to achieve success. In this chapter, we will explore how cultivating resilience and persistence with a can-do attitude can help you overcome any obstacle that comes your way.

What is Resilience?

Resilience is the ability to bounce back from difficult situations. It is the ability to overcome adversity, trauma, and stress and continue to move forward. Resilience is a key trait that helps people succeed in all areas of life. Whether you are facing a personal challenge or a professional setback, resilience will help you persevere and come out stronger on the other side.

Cultivating Resilience with a Can-Do Attitude

A can-do attitude is a positive mindset that focuses on solutions rather than problems. It is an attitude that says, "I can do this" rather than "I can't do this." Cultivating a can-do attitude can help you build resilience by helping you stay optimistic and motivated in the face of adversity.

Here are some tips for cultivating resilience with a can-do attitude:

Focus on Solutions

When faced with a challenge, it can be easy to get stuck in the problem. However, a can-do attitude focuses on finding solutions rather than dwelling on the problem. Instead of asking, "Why did this happen?" ask, "What can I do to fix it?" This mindset shift can help you find solutions to even the most challenging problems.

Stay Optimistic

Optimism is a key trait of a can-do attitude. When faced with a setback, it can be easy to feel discouraged and give up. However, a can-do attitude focuses on the positive and looks for the silver lining in every situation. By staying optimistic, you can maintain your motivation and focus on your goals, even in the face of adversity.

Practice Self-Care

Resilience requires physical and emotional strength. Practicing self-care, such as getting enough sleep, eating a healthy diet, and exercising regularly, can help you build the physical and emotional resilience you need to overcome challenges.

Build a Support System

No one can go through life alone. Building a support system of friends, family, and colleagues can provide you with the emotional support you need when facing challenges. A can-do attitude acknowledges that it's okay to ask for help and seeks out the support of others when needed.

What is Persistence?

Persistence is the ability to keep going, even in the face of obstacles and setbacks. It is the willingness to put in the time and effort required to achieve a goal, even when the going gets tough. Persistence is a critical trait that helps people achieve success in all areas of life.

10: CULTIVATING RESILIENCE AND PERSISTENCE WITH A CAN-DO ATTITUDE

Cultivating Persistence with a Can-Do Attitude

A can-do attitude is a powerful tool for cultivating persistence. When you believe that you can achieve your goals, even in the face of obstacles, you are more likely to keep going. Here are some tips for cultivating persistence with a can-do attitude:

Set Realistic Goals

Setting realistic goals is essential for cultivating persistence. When your goals are unrealistic, it can be easy to get discouraged and give up. However, when you set achievable goals, you can stay motivated and focused, even when facing obstacles.

Break Goals into Manageable Tasks

Breaking your goals into manageable tasks can make them feel more achievable. When you have a clear plan for achieving your goals, it can be easier to stay focused and motivated, even when facing setbacks.

Celebrate Small Wins

10: CULTIVATING RESILIENCE AND PERSISTENCE WITH A CAN-DO ATTITUDE

Celebrating small wins can help you stay motivated and focused on your goals. When you achieve a small win, take the time to acknowledge your progress and pat yourself on the back. This can help you build momentum and stay motivated as you work towards your larger goals.

Stay Flexible

Persistence requires a willingness to adapt and be flexible. When faced with obstacles or setbacks, it's important to be open to trying new approaches and adjusting your plan as needed. A can-do attitude encourages flexibility and a willingness to keep trying until you find what works.

Learn from Failure

Failure is a natural part of the learning process. When faced with failure, it's important to reflect on what went wrong and use that information to make changes and improve your approach. A can-do attitude sees failure as an opportunity to learn and grow, rather than a reason to give up.

The Power of a Can-Do Attitude

Cultivating resilience and persistence with a can-do attitude can help you overcome any obstacle that comes your way. When you believe in yourself and your ability to overcome challenges, you are more likely to stay motivated and focused, even in the face of setbacks. By focusing on solutions, staying optimistic, practicing self-care, building a support system, setting realistic goals, breaking goals into manageable tasks, celebrating small wins, staying flexible, and learning from failure, you can cultivate the mindset of winners and achieve unprecedented success in all areas of your life.

In conclusion, a can-do attitude is a powerful tool for achieving success and overcoming obstacles. By cultivating resilience and persistence with a can-do attitude, you can overcome any challenge that comes your way and achieve your goals. Remember, success is not about being perfect; it's about having the mindset and determination to keep going, even when the going gets tough. So, believe in yourself, stay focused on your goals, and never give up on your dreams. With a can-do attitude, anything is possible!

11: The Role of Visualization and Positive Thinking in a Can-Do Attitude

Visualization and positive thinking play a crucial role in developing and maintaining a can-do attitude. They help us tap into our innate potential and unlock our true capabilities. In this chapter, we will explore the science behind visualization and positive thinking, their benefits, and practical tips to incorporate them into our daily lives.

What is Visualization?

Visualization, also known as mental imagery, is a powerful technique that involves creating vivid and detailed mental images of desired outcomes. It is based on the idea that our thoughts and imagination have the power to influence our physical reality.

When we visualize, we activate the same neural pathways in our brain as when we actually perform the action. This leads to the release of neurochemicals, such as dopamine and serotonin, which promote feelings of happiness, motivation, and focus.

11: THE ROLE OF VISUALIZATION AND POSITIVE THINKING IN A CAN-DO ATTITUDE

Visualization can be used in various areas of life, such as sports, business, and personal development. Athletes, for example, use visualization to mentally rehearse their performance and improve their skills. Entrepreneurs use it to envision their goals and create a roadmap for success. And individuals use it to overcome fears, phobias, and limiting beliefs.

Benefits of Visualization

The benefits of visualization are numerous and far-reaching. Some of the most notable ones include:

Improved performance: Visualization can enhance performance by improving focus, confidence, and motivation. By mentally rehearsing an activity, we become more familiar and comfortable with it, leading to better results.

Reduced stress: Visualization can reduce stress and anxiety by activating the relaxation response in our bodies. When we visualize peaceful and calming scenes, our bodies respond by slowing down our heart rate and reducing tension.

Increased creativity: Visualization can stimulate our creativity and imagination, leading to innovative ideas and solutions.

Increased resilience: Visualization can help us develop a more positive and resilient mindset, which can help us bounce back from setbacks and challenges.

Tips for Effective Visualization

To get the most out of visualization, there are a few tips and techniques to keep in mind:

Start with a clear goal: Before you begin visualizing, it's important to have a clear and specific goal in mind. What do you want to achieve? What does success look like? The more specific and detailed your goal, the easier it will be to visualize.

Use all your senses: When visualizing, try to engage all your senses. What does the scene look, sound, smell, taste, and feel like? The more sensory information you can include, the more vivid and effective your visualization will be.

Practice regularly: Like any skill, visualization takes practice. Make it a habit to visualize your goals and desires every day, preferably at the same time and in a quiet and comfortable space.

Stay positive: When visualizing, focus on positive outcomes and feelings. Avoid negative thoughts and doubts, as they can sabotage your efforts and limit your potential.

What is Positive Thinking?

Positive thinking is a mindset that emphasizes the power of positive thoughts and beliefs. It is based on the idea that our thoughts and emotions have a profound impact on our physical and mental health, relationships, and overall well-being.

Positive thinking involves cultivating a positive attitude towards life, focusing on the good in every situation, and reframing negative thoughts into positive ones. It doesn't mean ignoring problems or denying reality, but rather approaching them with a positive and optimistic mindset.

Benefits of Positive Thinking

The benefits of positive thinking are vast and well-documented. Here are some of the most significant ones:

11: THE ROLE OF VISUALIZATION AND POSITIVE THINKING IN A CAN-DO ATTITUDE

Improved mental health: Positive thinking can reduce symptoms of anxiety and depression, boost self-esteem and confidence, and promote a sense of well-being and happiness.

Improved physical health: Positive thinking can improve physical health by reducing stress, lowering blood pressure, and boosting the immune system.

Improved relationships: Positive thinking can enhance relationships by improving communication, empathy, and understanding. It can also attract positive and supportive people into our lives.

Improved performance: Positive thinking can improve performance in various areas, such as academics, sports, and business. It can boost motivation, confidence, and focus, leading to better results.

Tips for Positive Thinking

Here are some tips and techniques for cultivating a positive mindset:

Practice gratitude: Gratitude is a powerful tool for positive thinking. Focus on the good in your life and express gratitude for it regularly. This can be done through journaling, meditation, or simply acknowledging and appreciating the people and things in your life.

Reframe negative thoughts: When negative thoughts arise, try to reframe them into positive ones. For example, instead of thinking "I can't do this," think "I am capable and resourceful, and I can find a way to do this."

Surround yourself with positivity: Surround yourself with positive and supportive people, and seek out positive media and information. Limit exposure to negative news and media.

Practice positive self-talk: Speak to yourself in a positive and encouraging way. Avoid negative self-talk and self-criticism.

Visualize positive outcomes: Use visualization techniques to imagine positive outcomes and feelings. This can boost confidence and motivation, and help overcome fears and doubts.

11: THE ROLE OF VISUALIZATION AND POSITIVE THINKING IN A CAN-DO ATTITUDE

Incorporating Visualization and Positive Thinking into a Can-Do Attitude

Visualization and positive thinking are powerful tools for cultivating a can-do attitude. By imagining positive outcomes and beliefs, we can tap into our innate potential and unlock our true capabilities.

Here are some practical tips for incorporating visualization and positive thinking into a can-do attitude:

Set clear and specific goals: Before visualizing, set clear and specific goals that align with your values and aspirations.

Visualize yourself achieving your goals: Use mental imagery to visualize yourself achieving your goals. Imagine the process and the outcome in vivid detail, engaging all your senses.

Believe in yourself: Believe that you are capable and deserving of achieving your goals. Cultivate a positive and confident mindset, and reframe negative thoughts into positive ones.

Take action: Visualization and positive thinking are power-

ful, but they are not enough on their own. Take action towards your goals, and use your positive mindset to fuel your
efforts.

Practice regularly: Visualization and positive thinking are
skills that require regular practice. Make them a part of
your daily routine, and be patient and persistent in your efforts.

Conclusion

Visualization and positive thinking are essential components of a can-do attitude. They can help us tap into our potential, overcome limiting beliefs, and achieve unprecedented success in all areas of life.

By setting clear goals, visualizing positive outcomes, cultivating a positive mindset, and taking action, we can unlock
our true capabilities and achieve our greatest aspirations.
So, go ahead and embrace the power of visualization and
positive thinking, and unlock your true potential today!

12: Building Confidence with a Can-Do Attitude

Confidence is a powerful force that can take you places you never thought possible. With confidence, you can take on challenges that you would normally shy away from, push yourself to reach new heights, and achieve your goals with ease. However, building confidence is not always easy, and many people struggle with self-doubt and a lack of belief in their own abilities. That's where a can-do attitude comes in - it's a mindset that can help you build the confidence you need to succeed in all areas of your life.

What is a Can-Do Attitude?

A can-do attitude is a mindset that is characterized by a positive outlook and a belief that anything is possible. It is a way of thinking that focuses on solutions rather than problems, and it is characterized by a willingness to take on challenges and try new things.

People with a can-do attitude are not afraid to fail, because they know that failure is just a temporary setback on the road to success. They are resilient in the face of adversity, and they don't give up easily. Instead, they see every challenge as an opportunity to learn and grow, and they use set-backs as motivation to work even harder.

Why is a Can-Do Attitude Important for Building Confidence?

Confidence is a key ingredient in success, and a can-do attitude is essential for building confidence. When you believe that you can accomplish anything you set your mind to, you are more likely to take risks and try new things. You are also more likely to bounce back from setbacks and keep going, even when things get tough.

On the other hand, when you have a negative mindset and a lack of belief in your own abilities, you are more likely to give up at the first sign of difficulty. You may also be more prone to anxiety and stress, which can further erode your confidence and hold you back from achieving your goals.

How to Build Confidence with a Can-Do Attitude

Building confidence with a can-do attitude is not something that happens overnight - it takes time, effort, and practice. However, with the right mindset and approach, anyone can develop the confidence they need to succeed. Here are some tips for building confidence with a can-do attitude:

Challenge Your Limiting Beliefs

Many people struggle with self-doubt and limiting beliefs that hold them back from achieving their full potential. These beliefs may be based on past experiences, negative feedback from others, or simply a lack of confidence in their own abilities.

To build confidence with a can-do attitude, it's important to challenge these limiting beliefs and replace them with more positive, empowering beliefs. For example, instead of telling yourself "I'm not good enough," try saying "I am capable of learning and improving." By reframing your thoughts in a more positive way, you can begin to shift your mindset and build confidence in your abilities.

Take Small Steps

Building confidence is all about taking action, but it's important to start small and work your way up. Instead of trying to tackle a huge goal all at once, break it down into smaller, more manageable steps. This will help you build momentum and gradually increase your confidence as you achieve each small victory.

For example, if you want to start a new business, you might start by doing some research, creating a business plan, and networking with other entrepreneurs. As you achieve each small goal, your confidence will grow, and you'll be better equipped to take on bigger challenges.

Embrace Failure as a Learning Opportunity

Failure is a natural part of the learning process, and it's important to embrace it as a learning opportunity rather than a reason to give up. When you experience setbacks or failures, take the time to reflect on what went wrong and what you can learn from the experience.

By reframing failure as a valuable learning opportunity, you can turn it into a source of motivation and inspiration. Use the lessons you learn from your failures to improve your skills, adjust your approach, and try again with renewed confidence and determination.

12: BUILDING CONFIDENCE WITH A CAN-DO ATTITUDE

Practice Positive Self-Talk

The way you talk to yourself can have a big impact on your confidence and overall mindset. If you're constantly telling yourself negative things, you're likely to feel anxious, stressed, and discouraged. On the other hand, if you practice positive self-talk, you can boost your confidence and cultivate a can-do attitude.

To practice positive self-talk, start by noticing when you're being overly critical or negative. When you catch yourself thinking negative thoughts, try to reframe them in a more positive way. For example, instead of thinking "I'll never be able to do this," try thinking "This is challenging, but I can figure it out with some effort and determination."

Surround Yourself with Positive People

The people you spend time with can have a big impact on your mindset and confidence. If you're constantly around negative, pessimistic people, it's likely to rub off on you and erode your own sense of confidence. On the other hand, if you surround yourself with positive, supportive people, you'll be more likely to adopt a can-do attitude and build your confidence.

Take some time to evaluate the people in your life and con-
sider how they impact your mindset. If there are people who
consistently bring you down or discourage you, try to limit
your time with them or find more positive, uplifting people
to spend time with instead.

Celebrate Your Successes

Finally, it's important to celebrate your successes, no matter
how small they may be. When you achieve a goal or make
progress towards something you've been working on, take
the time to acknowledge and celebrate your success. This
will help you build momentum and reinforce your belief in
your own abilities.

Celebrating your successes can take many forms, from
treating yourself to something you enjoy to sharing your accomplishment with friends and family. The key is to acknowledge your hard work and give yourself credit for your
achievements.

In conclusion, building confidence with a can-do attitude is a process that takes time, effort, and practice. By challenging your limiting beliefs, taking small steps, embracing failure as a learning opportunity, practicing positive self-talk, surrounding yourself with positive people, and celebrating your successes, you can cultivate a can-do attitude and build the confidence you need to achieve your goals and unlock your true potential.

13: Staying Motivated with a Can-Do Attitude

Motivation is the driving force behind success. It's the fire that fuels our passion and pushes us to overcome obstacles, achieve our goals, and reach new heights. Without motivation, even the most talented individuals can fall short of their potential.

Staying motivated, however, is not always easy. Life can throw us curveballs, and it's easy to become discouraged or lose our enthusiasm. But with the power of a can-do attitude, we can maintain our motivation and keep moving forward, no matter what challenges we may face.

So, how do we stay motivated with a can-do attitude? Here are some tips to help you cultivate the mindset of a winner and unlock your true potential.

Set Clear Goals

One of the most effective ways to stay motivated is to set clear goals for yourself. Goals give you direction and purpose, and they help you measure your progress and celebrate your successes. Make sure your goals are specific, measurable, achievable, relevant, and time-bound (SMART). Write them down and review them regularly, so you stay focused and committed.

Visualize Your Success

Visualization is a powerful tool for staying motivated. Take some time each day to visualize yourself achieving your goals. See yourself succeeding, feeling happy, and enjoying the rewards of your hard work. This positive visualization will help you stay motivated and focused, even during tough times.

Celebrate Small Wins

Don't wait for big successes to celebrate. Celebrate small wins along the way, too. Acknowledge your progress, and reward yourself for your efforts. This positive reinforcement will boost your confidence and keep you motivated to keep going.

Surround Yourself with Positivity

Negative thoughts and people can drain your motivation and sap your energy. Surround yourself with positive influences instead. Spend time with people who inspire and support you, read books and articles that uplift you, and listen to music or podcasts that motivate you.

Embrace Failure

Failure is a natural part of the learning process. Don't be afraid to fail. Instead, embrace it as an opportunity to learn and grow. When you make mistakes, reflect on what you can do differently next time, and keep moving forward with a positive attitude.

Keep Learning

Never stop learning. The more you know, the more you can do. Read books, take courses, attend workshops, and seek out mentors who can teach you new skills and perspectives. This continuous learning will keep you motivated and engaged in your pursuits.

Focus on Your Why

What drives you? What motivates you to keep going, even when things get tough? Focus on your why – your deeper purpose and passion – to stay motivated and energized.

13: STAYING MOTIVATED WITH A CAN-DO ATTITUDE

When you know why you're doing something, you'll be more committed to seeing it through.

Take Care of Yourself

Self-care is essential for staying motivated. Take care of your physical, emotional, and mental health by getting enough sleep, eating well, exercising regularly, and taking breaks when you need them. When you feel good, you'll have more energy and motivation to tackle your goals.

Keep a Positive Attitude

A positive attitude is essential for maintaining a can-do attitude. Even when things get tough, look for the silver lining and focus on the positives. Believe in yourself, and trust that you have what it takes to succeed.

Stay Persistent

Finally, stay persistent. Success rarely comes overnight. It takes time, effort, and patience to achieve your goals. Stay focused, stay committed, and keep moving forward, even when progress is slow. With a can-do attitude, you can overcome any obstacle and achieve your dreams.

In conclusion, staying motivated with a can-do attitude is all about cultivating a positive mindset, setting clear goals, surrounding yourself with positivity, embracing failure, and taking care of yourself. It's not always easy, but with practice, it can become a habit that leads to unprecedented success in all areas of life.

Remember, motivation is not just about the end result, but also the journey towards it. It's about enjoying the process, learning from your mistakes, and celebrating your progress along the way. With a can-do attitude, you can turn challenges into opportunities, setbacks into lessons, and dreams into reality.

However, staying motivated is not a one-time effort, but an ongoing process. You will encounter obstacles and setbacks along the way that can test your resolve. But with a can-do attitude, you can turn these obstacles into opportunities to learn and grow, and come out stronger and more motivated than ever before.

It's also important to remember that motivation is not a finite resource. It's something that you can cultivate and grow over time. By implementing the tips discussed in this chapter, you can create a positive mindset that supports your motivation and leads to greater success.

Finally, it's essential to remember that a can-do attitude is not just about achieving success in one area of life, but about living a fulfilling and meaningful life in all areas. By embracing a can-do attitude, you can unlock your true potential and achieve unprecedented success in your personal and professional life.

So, go out there and embrace a can-do attitude! Set clear goals, surround yourself with positivity, stay persistent, and believe in yourself. With a can-do attitude, the possibilities are endless, and success is within your reach.

14: Embracing Failure and Learning from Mistakes with a Can-Do Attitude

Everyone has experienced failure at some point in their lives, whether it's a small setback or a significant loss. Failure is often seen as a negative and something to avoid at all costs, but in reality, it can be a powerful tool for growth and learning. In fact, some of the most successful people in history have experienced multiple failures before achieving their goals. It's not the failures themselves that define us, but rather how we choose to respond to them.

The first step in embracing failure and learning from mistakes is to shift our mindset. Instead of seeing failure as a personal reflection of our abilities or worth, we can view it as an opportunity for growth and improvement. This is where the can-do attitude comes into play. A can-do attitude is characterized by a willingness to take on challenges, a belief in one's ability to overcome obstacles, and a determination to learn from mistakes.

One way to cultivate a can-do attitude is to practice self-compassion. When we experience failure, it's easy to fall into a pattern of negative self-talk and self-criticism. However, this only serves to reinforce limiting beliefs and can prevent us from taking risks in the future. Instead, we can approach ourselves with kindness and understanding, recognizing that failure is a natural part of the learning process.

Another key aspect of embracing failure is to take ownership of our mistakes. It's easy to blame external factors or other people for our shortcomings, but this only serves to disempower us. When we take responsibility for our actions, we become empowered to make changes and improve our outcomes. This is not to say that external factors don't play a role in our success or failure, but rather that we have the power to control our own responses.

Once we have shifted our mindset and taken ownership of our mistakes, we can begin to learn from them. This requires a willingness to reflect on our experiences and identify areas for improvement. We can ask ourselves questions such as: What did I do well? What could I have done differently? What did I learn from this experience? By taking the time to reflect and learn from our mistakes, we can avoid repeating the same patterns in the future.

It's also important to remember that failure is not a one-time event. It's an ongoing process of experimentation and growth. Just as we don't expect to become experts in a new skill overnight, we shouldn't expect to avoid failure completely. Rather, we can adopt a growth mindset and view each setback as an opportunity to learn and improve.

Of course, embracing failure is easier said than done. It requires a certain level of vulnerability and a willingness to step outside of our comfort zones. However, the benefits of a can-do attitude are clear. By embracing failure and learning from our mistakes, we can unlock our true potential and achieve unprecedented success in all areas of life.

One example of a person who embodies a can-do attitude is Thomas Edison. Edison famously failed thousands of times before finally inventing the light bulb. When asked about his failures, he replied, "I have not failed. I've just found 10,000 ways that won't work." This attitude of persistence and determination allowed Edison to keep going despite numerous setbacks, and ultimately led to one of the most transformative inventions in history.

14: EMBRACING FAILURE AND LEARNING FROM MIS-TAKES WITH A CAN-DO ATTITUDE

In conclusion, embracing failure and learning from mistakes is a critical component of a can-do attitude. By shifting our mindset, taking ownership of our mistakes, reflecting on our experiences, and adopting a growth mindset, we can transform failure into a powerful tool for growth and learning. As we navigate the ups and downs of life, we can cultivate a can-do attitude that empowers us to achieve our goals and overcome any obstacle that comes our way.

15: Overcoming Fear and Taking Action with a Can-Do Attitude

The fear of failure is one of the biggest obstacles to success. It's a feeling that most people experience at some point in their lives. Fear can be paralyzing, preventing us from taking the necessary actions to achieve our goals and reach our full potential. However, with the right mindset and attitude, you can overcome fear and take action towards achieving your dreams.

In this chapter, we will explore the concept of a can-do attitude, and how it can help you overcome your fears and take action towards your goals. We will discuss the importance of mindset, the power of visualization, and the benefits of taking action. We will also explore practical techniques and exercises that you can use to cultivate a can-do attitude and overcome your fears.

The Power of Mindset

The first step in cultivating a can-do attitude is to develop a growth mindset. This means embracing the belief that you can learn, grow, and improve through hard work and dedication. People with a growth mindset see failure as an opportunity to learn and grow, rather than a sign of inadequacy.

On the other hand, people with a fixed mindset believe that their abilities and intelligence are set in stone. They see failure as a reflection of their inherent limitations, and may give up on their goals when faced with challenges.

To develop a growth mindset, start by reframing your beliefs about failure. Rather than seeing it as a personal failure, view it as an opportunity to learn and grow. Embrace challenges as opportunities to push yourself out of your comfort zone and develop new skills.

The Power of Visualization

Visualization is a powerful tool that can help you overcome your fears and take action towards your goals. By visualizing yourself succeeding, you can increase your confidence, motivation, and resilience.

To use visualization effectively, start by setting a clear goal for yourself. Visualize yourself achieving that goal, and imagine the feeling of accomplishment and satisfaction that comes with it. Visualize the steps you will take to achieve your goal, and imagine yourself overcoming any obstacles that may arise along the way.

Visualization is most effective when done consistently over time. Take a few minutes each day to visualize yourself achieving your goal, and allow yourself to fully immerse in the feeling of success.

The Benefits of Taking Action

Taking action is the most important step in overcoming your fears and achieving your goals. Action is the only way to turn your dreams into reality.

When you take action, you build momentum towards your goals. Each small step you take towards your goal increases your confidence and motivation, and brings you closer to your ultimate destination.

In addition, taking action helps you overcome your fears by showing you that you are capable of achieving your goals. Each time you take action towards your goal, you prove to yourself that you have what it takes to succeed.

Practical Techniques and Exercises

15: OVERCOMING FEAR AND TAKING ACTION WITH A CAN-DO ATTITUDE

To cultivate a can-do attitude and overcome your fears, try the following practical techniques and exercises:

Practice positive self-talk. Use affirmations and positive statements to reinforce your belief in yourself and your abilities.

Break your goal down into smaller, manageable steps. This makes your goal more achievable, and helps you build momentum towards your ultimate destination.

Take small, consistent action towards your goal each day. Even if it's just for a few minutes, taking action every day helps build momentum and increases your confidence.

Celebrate your successes, no matter how small. Acknowledge your progress and give yourself credit for the work you have done.

Surround yourself with positive, supportive people who believe in you and your goals. Their encouragement and support can be a powerful motivator when you are facing challenges.

Visualize yourself succeeding. Use the power of visualization to imagine yourself achieving your goals and overcoming any obstacles that may arise.

Conclusion

Overcoming fear and taking action towards your goals requires a can-do attitude and a growth mindset. By reframing your beliefs about failure, embracing challenges, and visualizing your success, you can increase your confidence, motivation, and resilience.

Taking action is the most important step in achieving your goals. Each small step you take towards your goal increases your momentum and brings you closer to your destination. By practicing positive self-talk, breaking your goal down into smaller steps, and taking small, consistent action each day, you can build momentum towards your goals.

It's important to celebrate your successes along the way, no matter how small. Acknowledge your progress and give yourself credit for the work you have done. Surround yourself with positive, supportive people who believe in you and your goals. Their encouragement and support can be a powerful motivator when you are facing challenges.

15: OVERCOMING FEAR AND TAKING ACTION WITH A CAN-DO ATTITUDE

Remember, cultivating a can-do attitude is not an overnight process. It takes time, dedication, and persistence. But with the right mindset and attitude, you can overcome your fears and achieve your goals. So, believe in yourself, take action, and never give up on your dreams. With a can-do attitude, anything is possible.

16: The Importance of Self-Care in Maintaining a Can-Do Attitude

Introduction

In today's fast-paced world, it is easy to get caught up in the hustle and bustle of daily life. We often prioritize our work, family, and social obligations over our own well-being. However, neglecting our own self-care can have detrimental effects on our physical, emotional, and mental health. In this chapter, we will explore the importance of self-care in maintaining a can-do attitude, and how it can help you unlock your true potential and achieve unprecedented success in all areas of your life.

What is self-care?

Self-care refers to any activity that we engage in to take care of our physical, emotional, and mental health. It can be as simple as taking a warm bath or going for a walk, or more complex like seeing a therapist or attending a meditation retreat. The key to self-care is that it is intentional and deliberate, and is done with the purpose of enhancing our overall well-being.

16: THE IMPORTANCE OF SELF-CARE IN MAINTAINING A CAN-DO ATTITUDE

Why is self-care important?

Self-care is essential for maintaining a can-do attitude because it helps us to recharge our batteries and replenish our energy reserves. When we neglect our own needs, we become physically and emotionally exhausted, which can lead to burnout, stress, and even depression. Self-care is also important because it helps us to cultivate self-love and self-compassion, which are essential for building a strong sense of self-worth and confidence.

The benefits of self-care

There are numerous benefits to practicing self-care on a regular basis. Here are just a few:

Increased productivity and focus: When we take care of our physical, emotional, and mental health, we are better able to concentrate and stay focused on our goals. This can lead to increased productivity and a greater sense of accomplishment.

Reduced stress and anxiety: Self-care practices like meditation, yoga, and deep breathing can help to reduce stress and anxiety, which are two major obstacles to maintaining a can-do attitude.

Improved physical health: Eating well, exercising regularly, and getting enough sleep are all important components of self-care, and can have a profound impact on our physical health.

Enhanced emotional well-being: Engaging in activities that bring us joy and fulfillment, like reading, painting, or spending time with loved ones, can help us to feel more emotionally balanced and content.

Increased self-esteem: When we take care of ourselves, we send a powerful message to ourselves and others that we are worthy of love and respect. This can help to boost our self-esteem and confidence, which are essential for maintaining a can-do attitude.

Tips for practicing self-care

Here are some tips for incorporating self-care into your daily routine:

Make it a priority: Set aside time each day for self-care, and treat it as a non-negotiable part of your schedule.

Choose activities that you enjoy: Self-care should be enjoyable and fulfilling, so choose activities that you genuinely look forward to.

Be mindful: When engaging in self-care activities, be fully present in the moment and focus on the sensations and emotions that arise.

Take care of your physical health: Eat well, exercise regularly, and get enough sleep to ensure that your body is functioning at its best.

Seek support when needed: If you are struggling with your mental health, don't hesitate to seek the help of a mental health professional.

Conclusion

In conclusion, self-care is an essential component of maintaining a can-do attitude and achieving unprecedented success in all areas of life. By prioritizing our own well-being, we are better able to recharge our batteries, cultivate self-love and compassion, and build the confidence and resilience necessary to overcome obstacles and achieve our goals. So, make self-care a priority in your daily routine, and watch as your can-do attitude and overall sense of well-being flourish. Remember, taking care of yourself is not a selfish act, but rather a necessary one in order to live a happy and fulfilled life.

It is important to note that self-care looks different for everyone, and there is no one-size-fits-all approach. What works for one person may not work for another. It is up to each individual to experiment and find the self-care practices that work best for them.

Additionally, practicing self-care does not mean that we will never experience challenges or setbacks. Life is full of ups and downs, and we will inevitably face difficult times. However, by prioritizing our own well-being, we are better equipped to handle these challenges and bounce back more quickly.

In order to maintain a can-do attitude, it is important to approach self-care with a positive and proactive mindset. Rather than viewing self-care as a chore or something that we "have to" do, we should approach it with a sense of excitement and anticipation. By embracing self-care as an opportunity to nourish ourselves, we can cultivate a can-do attitude that empowers us to tackle any obstacle that comes our way.

In conclusion, self-care is an essential component of maintaining a can-do attitude and achieving unprecedented success in all areas of life. By prioritizing our own well-being and practicing self-love and compassion, we can build the confidence and resilience necessary to overcome obstacles and achieve our goals. So, make self-care a priority in your daily routine, and watch as your can-do attitude and overall sense of well-being flourish. Remember, taking care of yourself is not a selfish act, but rather a necessary one in order to live a happy and fulfilled life.

17: The Role of Gratitude and Mindfulness in a Can-Do Attitude

As human beings, we are wired to focus on what we don't have rather than what we do have. We tend to concentrate on our problems and the things that are not going right in our lives, instead of appreciating what we have and the things that are going well. This negative focus can make us feel helpless, powerless, and demotivated, which can hinder our ability to achieve success and reach our full potential.

In order to cultivate a can-do attitude, it is essential to shift our focus from negativity to positivity. One way to do this is by practicing gratitude and mindfulness. Gratitude and mindfulness are powerful tools that can transform your mindset and help you develop a positive outlook on life. In this chapter, we will explore the role of gratitude and mindfulness in developing a can-do attitude and achieving unprecedented success in all areas of life.

Gratitude: The Attitude of Appreciation

Gratitude is the practice of appreciating what we have, rather than focusing on what we lack. When we cultivate a spirit of gratitude, we acknowledge and give thanks for the blessings in our lives, no matter how big or small they may be. This attitude of appreciation can have a profound impact on our mindset, our emotional well-being, and our relationships.

Gratitude can transform your mindset by shifting your focus from negativity to positivity. Instead of dwelling on the problems and challenges in your life, you begin to focus on the good things that are happening. This positive shift in perspective can boost your self-esteem, increase your motivation, and improve your overall well-being.

In addition, practicing gratitude can help you develop stronger and more meaningful relationships. When you express gratitude towards others, you are acknowledging their positive impact on your life. This expression of appreciation can deepen your connections with others and enhance your sense of community.

Gratitude is also a powerful antidote to negative emotions such as fear, anxiety, and depression. When we focus on what we are grateful for, we activate the part of our brain that is associated with positive emotions, which can help to counteract negative feelings.

17: THE ROLE OF GRATITUDE AND MINDFULNESS IN A CAN-DO ATTITUDE

To cultivate a spirit of gratitude, it is important to make it a daily practice. One way to do this is by keeping a gratitude journal. Each day, write down three things that you are grateful for. They can be simple things, such as the warm sun on your face or the taste of your favorite food, or they can be more profound, such as the love of your family or the opportunity to pursue your dreams.

Another way to cultivate gratitude is by expressing your appreciation to others. Take the time to thank the people in your life who have made a positive impact on you. It could be a friend who listened when you needed to talk, a teacher who inspired you to pursue your passions, or a mentor who helped you navigate a difficult situation.

Mindfulness: The Power of Presence

Mindfulness is the practice of being fully present in the moment, without judgment or distraction. When we practice mindfulness, we focus our attention on the present moment, without getting caught up in worries about the past or fears about the future. This presence can have a profound impact on our mindset, our emotional well-being, and our relationships.

17: THE ROLE OF GRATITUDE AND MINDFULNESS IN A CAN-DO ATTITUDE

Mindfulness can transform your mindset by helping you to become more aware of your thoughts and emotions. When you are mindful, you observe your thoughts and feelings without judgment, which can help you to recognize and let go of negative patterns of thinking. This increased self-awareness can also help you to make more conscious choices about how you respond to situations, rather than reacting automatically.

In addition, practicing mindfulness can help to reduce stress and anxiety. When we are mindful, we are less likely to get caught up in worries and fears about the future, which can help to reduce feelings of anxiety. Mindfulness can also help us to manage our emotions more effectively, allowing us to respond to situations with greater clarity and calmness.

Mindfulness can also improve our relationships by helping us to become more present and attentive to others. When we practice mindfulness, we are more able to listen deeply to others and respond with empathy and compassion. This can help to deepen our connections with others and improve our communication.

17: THE ROLE OF GRATITUDE AND MINDFULNESS IN A CAN-DO ATTITUDE

To cultivate mindfulness, it is important to make it a daily practice. One way to do this is by incorporating mindfulness meditation into your daily routine. This can be as simple as taking a few minutes each day to sit in quiet reflection, focusing on your breath and observing your thoughts without judgment.

Another way to cultivate mindfulness is by bringing mindful awareness to your daily activities. Whether it's washing dishes, walking in nature, or having a conversation with a friend, try to bring your full attention to the present moment, noticing the sights, sounds, and sensations around you.

Gratitude and Mindfulness: A Powerful Combination

Gratitude and mindfulness are powerful tools that can transform your mindset and help you to develop a can-do attitude. When practiced together, they can amplify their effects, leading to greater emotional well-being, stronger relationships, and increased motivation and success.

By cultivating a spirit of gratitude, you develop a mindset of appreciation and positivity. This positive mindset can help you to overcome challenges and setbacks, and to focus on the opportunities and possibilities that lie ahead.

By practicing mindfulness, you become more present and self-aware, allowing you to respond to situations with greater clarity and calmness. This increased awareness can also help you to recognize and let go of negative patterns of thinking, allowing you to develop a more positive and can-do attitude.

Together, gratitude and mindfulness can help you to unlock your true potential and achieve unprecedented success in all areas of life. By focusing on the present moment and appreciating the blessings in your life, you can cultivate a mindset of abundance and possibility, and achieve your dreams with a can-do attitude.

18: Developing Emotional Intelligence with a Can-Do Attitude

Emotional intelligence is a crucial aspect of personal and professional success. It refers to the ability to recognize, understand, and manage our emotions, as well as the emotions of others. Emotional intelligence enables us to communicate effectively, build strong relationships, and make better decisions.

In this chapter, we'll explore how developing emotional intelligence with a can-do attitude can help you unlock your true potential and achieve unprecedented success in all areas of life.

What is Emotional Intelligence?

Emotional intelligence, or EQ, is the ability to recognize and manage our emotions, as well as the emotions of others. It encompasses four key skills:

Self-awareness: The ability to recognize and understand your own emotions and how they affect your thoughts and behaviors.

Self-management: The ability to regulate your emotions and

behavior in a way that is positive and productive.

Social awareness: The ability to recognize and understand the emotions of others, and to respond appropriately to their emotional cues.

Relationship management: The ability to build and maintain strong relationships with others, based on trust, empathy, and effective communication.

Why is Emotional Intelligence Important?

Emotional intelligence is critical to personal and professional success for several reasons:

Improved communication: Emotional intelligence helps us communicate effectively with others, both verbally and non-verbally. It enables us to understand and respond to the emotional needs of others, which can help us build stronger relationships and avoid misunderstandings.

Better decision-making: Emotional intelligence enables us to think more clearly and make better decisions, based on our understanding of our own emotions and the emotions of others.

18: DEVELOPING EMOTIONAL INTELLIGENCE WITH A CAN-DO ATTITUDE

Increased resilience: Emotional intelligence helps us manage stress and difficult situations more effectively, which can increase our resilience and ability to bounce back from setbacks.

Enhanced leadership: Emotional intelligence is a key component of effective leadership. Leaders who are emotionally intelligent are better able to understand and motivate their team members, build trust, and create a positive work environment.

Developing Emotional Intelligence with a Can-Do Attitude

Now that we understand the importance of emotional intelligence, let's explore how we can develop it with a can-do attitude.

Practice self-awareness: Developing self-awareness is the first step towards developing emotional intelligence. Start by paying attention to your own emotions, and how they affect your thoughts and behavior. Be honest with yourself about your strengths and weaknesses, and seek feedback from others to gain a better understanding of how you are perceived.

18: DEVELOPING EMOTIONAL INTELLIGENCE WITH A CAN-DO ATTITUDE

Manage your emotions: Once you have a better understanding of your own emotions, focus on managing them in a way that is positive and productive. This might involve strategies such as deep breathing, meditation, or exercise. It's also important to recognize when you need to take a break or step back from a situation to avoid becoming overwhelmed.

Practice empathy: Empathy is a key component of social awareness, and involves understanding and responding to the emotions of others. Practice active listening, and try to put yourself in the other person's shoes. Avoid making assumptions or judgments, and instead focus on understanding their perspective.

Build strong relationships: Relationship management is another key component of emotional intelligence. Focus on building strong, positive relationships with others based on trust, respect, and effective communication. Be open and honest, and take the time to listen to others and understand their needs.

Embrace a can-do attitude: Finally, developing emotional intelligence requires a positive, can-do attitude. This means approaching challenges and setbacks with optimism and resilience, and focusing on solutions rather than problems. Cultivate a growth mindset, and be willing to learn from your mistakes and try new approaches.

Conclusion

Developing emotional intelligence with a can-do attitude is critical to achieving personal and professional success. By focusing on self-awareness, managing your emotions, practicing empathy, building strong relationships, and embracing a can-do attitude, you can cultivate the mindset of winners and unlock your true potential in all areas of life.

Remember, developing emotional intelligence is a lifelong journey, and it requires ongoing practice and self-reflection. Be patient with yourself, and celebrate your progress along the way. With a can-do attitude and a commitment to personal growth, you can achieve unprecedented success and become the best version of yourself.

In the next chapter, we'll explore how a can-do attitude can help you overcome limiting beliefs and achieve your goals. We'll dive into strategies for shifting your mindset, setting meaningful goals, and taking action towards your dreams.

18: DEVELOPING EMOTIONAL INTELLIGENCE WITH A CAN-DO ATTITUDE

Stay tuned for an empowering and actionable guide to unlocking your full potential with the power of a can-do attitude!

19: The Connection between a Can-Do Attitude and Leadership

Leadership is an integral part of our lives. We all encounter leadership in one form or another, whether it's at work, school, or even in our personal lives. Some people are born leaders, while others develop their leadership skills over time. The good news is that regardless of your natural leadership abilities, you can always improve your leadership skills with the right attitude and mindset. In this chapter, we will explore the connection between a can-do attitude and leadership and how developing a can-do attitude can help you become a more effective leader.

A can-do attitude is a positive mindset that helps you approach challenges and opportunities with confidence and enthusiasm. It's the belief that you can accomplish anything you set your mind to, no matter how difficult or impossible it may seem. A can-do attitude is characterized by optimism, resilience, and a willingness to take risks and embrace change. It's a mindset that helps you overcome obstacles, stay motivated, and inspire others to achieve their goals.

Leadership, on the other hand, is the ability to inspire and influence others to work together towards a common goal.

19: THE CONNECTION BETWEEN A CAN-DO ATTITUDE AND LEADERSHIP

Effective leaders are able to communicate their vision and goals clearly, motivate their team, and create a positive work environment that fosters growth and development. Leaders are also responsible for making tough decisions, managing conflicts, and taking calculated risks.

The connection between a can-do attitude and leadership is clear. A can-do attitude is essential for effective leadership because it helps you approach challenges and opportunities with confidence and enthusiasm. As a leader, you must be able to inspire and motivate your team, and a can-do attitude can help you do just that. When you approach challenges with a positive attitude, you inspire your team to do the same. Your positive attitude becomes contagious, and your team is more likely to believe in themselves and their ability to achieve success.

A can-do attitude is also essential for overcoming obstacles and persevering through difficult times. As a leader, you will undoubtedly face challenges and setbacks, and a can-do attitude can help you stay motivated and focused on your goals. When you encounter obstacles, instead of giving up, you'll be more likely to find creative solutions and keep pushing forward. This kind of resilience is essential for effective leadership.

Another important aspect of a can-do attitude in leadership is the willingness to take risks and embrace change. As a leader, you must be willing to take calculated risks and make tough decisions that may not always be popular. You must also be open to change and willing to adapt to new situations and challenges. A can-do attitude can help you approach these situations with confidence and enthusiasm, which will inspire your team to do the same.

Developing a can-do attitude takes time and effort, but it's worth it. Here are some tips for cultivating a can-do attitude and becoming a more effective leader:

Focus on the positive: Instead of dwelling on the negative aspects of a situation, focus on the positive. Look for the opportunities and possibilities, and approach challenges with a positive attitude.

Embrace failure: Failure is a natural part of the learning process. Instead of fearing failure, embrace it as an opportunity to learn and grow. Use your failures as a stepping stone to success.

Take risks: Don't be afraid to take calculated risks. Remember that without risk, there can be no reward. Be willing to step outside of your comfort zone and try new things.

Stay motivated: It's easy to lose motivation when faced with challenges and setbacks. Keep yourself motivated by setting clear goals and tracking your progress. Celebrate your successes along the way.

Communicate clearly: Effective communication is essential for effective leadership. Be clear and concise when communicating your vision and goals to your team.

Lead by example: As a leader, you must lead by example. Demonstrate the behavior and attitude you expect from your team. If you want your team to have a can-do attitude, then you must have one yourself.

Encourage creativity: Encourage your team to think outside of the box and come up with creative solutions to problems. Create an environment that fosters creativity and innovation.

19: THE CONNECTION BETWEEN A CAN-DO ATTITUDE AND LEADERSHIP

Emphasize teamwork: Effective leadership is about bringing people together to achieve a common goal. Emphasize the importance of teamwork and collaboration, and create a positive work environment that fosters cooperation and mutual respect.

Learn from mistakes: No one is perfect, and everyone makes mistakes. When you make a mistake, acknowledge it, learn from it, and move on. Use your mistakes as an opportunity to grow and improve.

Stay humble: Effective leaders are humble and recognize that they don't have all the answers. Be open to feedback and criticism, and seek out the opinions and ideas of others.

In conclusion, a can-do attitude is essential for effective leadership. By cultivating a positive mindset, embracing failure, taking risks, staying motivated, communicating clearly, leading by example, encouraging creativity, emphasizing teamwork, learning from mistakes, and staying humble, you can become a more effective leader and inspire your team to achieve unprecedented success. Remember, leadership is not about having all the answers; it's about inspiring and influencing others to work together towards a common goal. With a can-do attitude, anything is possible!

20: Creating a Positive Culture with a Can-Do Attitude

In today's world, success is often determined by one's mindset. A positive attitude can take you a long way, and it's no wonder that people with a can-do attitude often outperform their peers. But how do you cultivate a can-do attitude? How do you create a positive culture in your workplace, in your family, and in your community? This chapter will explore the power of a can-do attitude and how to foster it in yourself and those around you.

What is a Can-Do Attitude?

A can-do attitude is a positive mindset that embraces challenges, embraces opportunities, and believes in the possibility of success. People with a can-do attitude are resilient, motivated, and self-assured. They don't let setbacks or obstacles get in their way, and they are willing to take risks to achieve their goals. A can-do attitude is not about being blindly optimistic or ignoring reality; it's about being realistic and proactive in the face of adversity.

Why is a Can-Do Attitude Important?

20: CREATING A POSITIVE CULTURE WITH A CAN-DO ATTITUDE

A can-do attitude is essential for success in all areas of life. Whether you're starting a business, pursuing a career, or trying to improve your personal life, a positive mindset can make all the difference. Here are some of the benefits of having a can-do attitude:

Increased Resilience: People with a can-do attitude are more resilient to setbacks and challenges. They bounce back quickly and are more likely to learn from their mistakes.

Improved Creativity: A positive mindset can help you think more creatively and find innovative solutions to problems.

Enhanced Motivation: When you have a can-do attitude, you're more motivated to take action and pursue your goals.

Greater Confidence: A can-do attitude can boost your self-confidence and help you believe in your abilities.

Better Relationships: When you have a positive mindset, you're more likely to attract positive people and build strong relationships.

How to Cultivate a Can-Do Attitude

20: CREATING A POSITIVE CULTURE WITH A CAN-DO ATTITUDE

So, how do you develop a can-do attitude? Here are some tips:

Identify and Challenge Limiting Beliefs: Limiting beliefs are the negative thoughts and beliefs that hold you back. To cultivate a can-do attitude, you need to identify these limiting beliefs and challenge them. Ask yourself, "Is this belief really true?" and "How can I reframe this belief in a positive way?"

Practice Gratitude: Gratitude is a powerful tool for cultivating a positive mindset. Take time each day to reflect on what you're grateful for, and focus on the positive aspects of your life.

Embrace Failure: Failure is a natural part of the learning process. Don't let fear of failure hold you back. Instead, embrace failure as an opportunity to learn and grow.

Focus on Solutions: When faced with a problem, focus on finding solutions rather than dwelling on the problem itself. Ask yourself, "What can I do to fix this?"

Surround Yourself with Positive People: Positive people can

inspire and motivate you to be your best self. Surround yourself with people who have a can-do attitude and who support your goals.

Creating a Positive Culture with a Can-Do Attitude

Cultivating a can-do attitude is not just an individual pursuit; it's also about creating a positive culture in your workplace, family, and community. Here are some ways to foster a positive culture with a can-do attitude:

Lead by Example: As a leader, you set the tone for the culture of your organization or family. Model a can-do attitude by being positive, proactive, and solution-focused.

Encourage Risk-Taking: Encourage your team or family members to take calculated risks and try new things. Celebrate successes and learn from failures.

Recognize and Reward Success: Recognize and reward individuals who demonstrate a can-do attitude and achieve their goals. This reinforces the importance of positivity and hard work.

Provide Support and Resources: Offer support and re-

sources to help individuals develop a can-do attitude. This
could include training, coaching, or mentorship.

Foster Collaboration: Encourage collaboration and teamwork, as this can help individuals feel supported and motivated. This can also lead to more creative and innovative
solutions to problems.

Communicate Effectively: Clear and effective communication is key to creating a positive culture. Encourage open
and honest communication, and provide feedback that is
constructive and supportive.

Create a Positive Environment: Make sure your workplace
or family environment is positive and supportive. This could
include things like a comfortable and welcoming physical
space, access to resources and tools, and opportunities for
social connection.

In conclusion, cultivating a can-do attitude is a powerful
way to achieve success and happiness in all areas of life. By
challenging limiting beliefs, practicing gratitude, embracing
failure, and focusing on solutions, you can develop a positive mindset that will help you overcome obstacles and

achieve your goals. And by creating a positive culture in your workplace, family, and community, you can inspire and motivate others to do the same. Remember, with a can-do attitude, anything is possible!

21: Inspiring and Motivating Others with a Can-Do Attitude

As humans, we are social creatures. We rely on the support, encouragement, and motivation of others to achieve our goals and realize our dreams. Inspiring and motivating others is not only a powerful way to help others succeed, but it is also a way to unlock your true potential and cultivate the mindset of a winner. In this chapter, we will explore how you can inspire and motivate others with a can-do attitude, and how doing so can lead to unprecedented success in all areas of life.

Before we dive into the nitty-gritty of inspiring and motivating others, let's take a moment to define what we mean by a can-do attitude. A can-do attitude is a positive, proactive, and resilient mindset that enables individuals to overcome obstacles, challenges, and setbacks. It is a mindset that is characterized by a belief in oneself and a willingness to take risks, learn from failure, and persevere in the face of adversity. A can-do attitude is not just a vague and nebulous concept; it is a concrete and actionable way of thinking and behaving that can be learned and practiced.

So, how can you inspire and motivate others with a can-do

attitude? Let's explore some practical strategies and techniques.

Lead by Example

One of the most effective ways to inspire and motivate others is to lead by example. If you want others to adopt a can-do attitude, you need to embody that attitude yourself. You need to be proactive, positive, and resilient in your own life and work. When others see you taking risks, learning from failure, and persevering in the face of adversity, they are more likely to be inspired and motivated to do the same.

Encourage Risk-Taking

Taking risks is a crucial part of cultivating a can-do attitude. When we take risks, we step outside our comfort zone, and we challenge ourselves to grow and learn. As a leader, you should encourage others to take risks and try new things. Encourage your team members to take calculated risks, and provide them with the support and resources they need to succeed. When you create a culture of risk-taking, you empower your team members to embrace their potential and achieve unprecedented success.

21: INSPIRING AND MOTIVATING OTHERS WITH A CAN-DO ATTITUDE

Provide Feedback and Recognition

Feedback and recognition are powerful tools for motivating others. When you provide feedback, you help others learn and grow, and you show them that you care about their success. When you recognize their achievements, you acknowledge their hard work and dedication, and you inspire them to continue to strive for excellence. Be specific and timely in your feedback and recognition, and make sure that it is genuine and heartfelt.

Set Realistic Goals

Setting realistic goals is an essential part of cultivating a can-do attitude. When we set goals that are challenging but achievable, we are more likely to be motivated to achieve them. As a leader, you should work with your team members to set realistic goals that align with their strengths and interests. Break larger goals into smaller, more manageable tasks, and provide your team members with the resources and support they need to achieve success.

Celebrate Successes

21: INSPIRING AND MOTIVATING OTHERS WITH A CAN-DO ATTITUDE

Celebrating successes is an important part of motivating others. When we celebrate our successes, we feel a sense of pride and accomplishment, and we are more likely to be motivated to continue to work hard and achieve even more. As a leader, you should celebrate your team members' successes, no matter how small they may be. Take the time to acknowledge their achievements, and make sure that they feel valued and appreciated.

Foster a Positive and Supportive Environment

Finally, fostering a positive and supportive environment is crucial for inspiring and motivating others. When we work in a positive and supportive environment, we feel valued, supported, and motivated to succeed. As a leader, you should create a culture of positivity and support, where team members feel safe to express their ideas, share their opinions, and ask for help when needed. Encourage open and honest communication, and make sure that everyone feels included and heard.

In addition to these strategies, there are a few other key principles that can help you inspire and motivate others with a can-do attitude:

21: INSPIRING AND MOTIVATING OTHERS WITH A CAN-DO ATTITUDE

Believe in Others: To inspire and motivate others, you need to believe in them. Believe in their potential, their capabilities, and their dreams. When you believe in others, you empower them to believe in themselves and to achieve unprecedented success.

Be Empathetic: Empathy is the ability to understand and share the feelings of others. To inspire and motivate others, you need to be empathetic. You need to understand their struggles, their fears, and their aspirations. When you show empathy, you create a deeper connection with others, and you inspire them to achieve more than they thought possible.

Practice Patience: Inspiring and motivating others takes time and effort. You need to be patient and persistent, even when progress is slow. Don't give up on others, even when they struggle or fail. Keep encouraging them, supporting them, and providing feedback, and eventually, they will succeed.

Be Flexible: Not everyone responds to motivation and inspiration in the same way. To be an effective motivator, you need to be flexible and adapt your approach to suit the needs and preferences of each individual. Some people may respond better to praise, while others may prefer constructive criticism. Some may respond better to visual aids or demonstrations, while others may prefer written instructions. Be willing to adjust your approach to meet the unique needs of each team member.

In conclusion, inspiring and motivating others with a can-do attitude is an essential part of achieving unprecedented success in all areas of life. By leading by example, encouraging risk-taking, providing feedback and recognition, setting realistic goals, celebrating successes, fostering a positive and supportive environment, believing in others, being empathetic, practicing patience, and being flexible, you can empower others to achieve their full potential and cultivate the mindset of winners. Remember, success is not just about what you achieve; it's also about what you inspire others to achieve.

22: Using a Can-Do Attitude to Overcome Adversity

Life is not always a bed of roses. In fact, more often than not, it is filled with obstacles, challenges, and hardships. These adversities can come in many forms – personal, professional, financial, health-related, and more. They can be small and temporary or large and life-changing. But one thing is certain, everyone faces adversity at some point in their life.

When adversity strikes, it can be easy to give up or feel defeated. However, it is important to remember that adversity is a part of life and that it can be overcome. One of the most powerful tools for overcoming adversity is a can-do attitude.

A can-do attitude is a mindset that focuses on solutions, rather than problems. It is a mindset that believes that anything is possible with the right mindset, hard work, and determination. A can-do attitude is not about being unrealistic or ignoring challenges, but rather about believing in yourself and your ability to overcome obstacles.

So, how can you use a can-do attitude to overcome adversity? Here are some tips and strategies:

22: USING A CAN-DO ATTITUDE TO OVERCOME ADVERSITY

Believe in Yourself

The first step in developing a can-do attitude is to believe in yourself. You must believe that you have what it takes to overcome adversity and achieve your goals. This belief is not about being arrogant or overconfident, but rather about having faith in your abilities and potential.

One way to develop this belief is to focus on your strengths and accomplishments. Make a list of your strengths, talents, and achievements. Remind yourself of your successes and how you have overcome challenges in the past. This will help you build confidence in your abilities and remind you that you have what it takes to overcome adversity.

Focus on Solutions

When facing adversity, it can be easy to get stuck in the problem. However, a can-do attitude focuses on solutions, not problems. Instead of dwelling on the problem, focus on finding solutions. Ask yourself, "What can I do to overcome this challenge?" or "What steps can I take to move forward?"

22: USING A CAN-DO ATTITUDE TO OVERCOME AD-VERSITY

One strategy to help you focus on solutions is to break down the problem into smaller, more manageable steps. This will help you see the problem as a series of challenges that can be overcome, rather than one overwhelming obstacle.

Take Action

A can-do attitude is not just about thinking positively, but also about taking action. Once you have identified solutions, it is important to take action to overcome the challenge. This may involve trying new things, taking risks, or stepping outside of your comfort zone.

Taking action may also involve asking for help or support from others. Remember that you do not have to face adversity alone. Reach out to friends, family, or professionals for help and support.

Learn from Setbacks

Setbacks and failures are a natural part of life, and they can be discouraging. However, a can-do attitude sees setbacks as opportunities to learn and grow. When faced with a setback, take the time to reflect on what went wrong and what you can do differently next time.

Instead of dwelling on the failure, focus on what you have learned and how you can use that knowledge to overcome future challenges. This will help you develop resilience and perseverance, two important traits for overcoming adversity.

Stay Positive

A can-do attitude is characterized by positivity and optimism. When facing adversity, it can be easy to become negative and pessimistic. However, it is important to stay positive and focused on your goals.

One way to stay positive is to practice gratitude. Take the time to appreciate the good things in your life and focus on what you are thankful for. This will help you maintain a positive outlook and give you the strength to overcome adversity.

In conclusion, a can-do attitude is a powerful tool for overcoming adversity. By believing in yourself, focusing on solutions, taking action, learning from setbacks, and staying positive, you can overcome even the most challenging obstacles in your life.

It is important to remember that developing a can-do attitude takes time and effort. It is not something that happens overnight, but rather a mindset that is cultivated over time. However, with practice and persistence, you can develop the mindset of a winner and achieve unprecedented success in all areas of your life.

Another important aspect of using a can-do attitude to overcome adversity is to maintain a growth mindset. A growth mindset is a belief that your abilities and intelligence can be developed through hard work and dedication. This mindset helps you to see challenges as opportunities for growth and learning, rather than as obstacles to be avoided.

To develop a growth mindset, focus on learning and improvement, rather than on proving yourself. Embrace challenges as opportunities to learn and grow, and don't be afraid to make mistakes. Remember that every mistake is an opportunity to learn and improve.

Finally, it is important to surround yourself with positive, supportive people who believe in you and your potential. Seek out mentors, coaches, and friends who can help you stay focused on your goals and support you through the challenges and setbacks.

In summary, using a can-do attitude to overcome adversity requires a combination of belief in oneself, focusing on solutions, taking action, learning from setbacks, and staying positive. It also requires a growth mindset and a supportive community. With these tools and strategies, you can overcome any obstacle and achieve unprecedented success in all areas of your life.

23: The Power of Positive Relationships in a Can-Do Attitude

Relationships are an essential part of our lives, and they play a crucial role in shaping our attitudes, beliefs, and overall wellbeing. Whether it's personal or professional, our relationships can have a significant impact on our lives, and they can either help or hinder our progress towards achieving our goals.

In this chapter, we will explore the power of positive relationships in cultivating a can-do attitude. We will look at how positive relationships can help us overcome limiting beliefs, boost our confidence, and provide us with the support we need to achieve unprecedented success in all areas of life.

Understanding the Impact of Relationships on Our Attitude

The relationships we have with others can have a significant impact on our attitude towards life. Negative relationships can lead to negative thinking patterns and limiting beliefs, while positive relationships can help us cultivate a can-do attitude.

23: THE POWER OF POSITIVE RELATIONSHIPS IN A CAN-DO ATTITUDE

When we surround ourselves with people who believe in us, support us, and encourage us to pursue our dreams, we are more likely to adopt a positive mindset and believe in ourselves. On the other hand, when we surround ourselves with people who criticize us, doubt our abilities, and bring us down, we are more likely to adopt a negative mindset and develop limiting beliefs.

Therefore, it's crucial to evaluate the relationships we have in our lives and determine which ones are positive and which ones are negative. By identifying the relationships that are holding us back and making changes to improve them or distance ourselves from them, we can cultivate a more positive attitude towards life.

Overcoming Limiting Beliefs Through Positive Relationships

One of the biggest challenges we face in developing a can-do attitude is overcoming limiting beliefs. These are negative thoughts and beliefs we have about ourselves and our abilities that hold us back from achieving our goals.

Positive relationships can help us overcome limiting beliefs by providing us with the support and encouragement we need to challenge them. When we surround ourselves with people who believe in us, we are more likely to challenge our limiting beliefs and push ourselves to achieve our goals.

For example, if you have a limiting belief that you're not good enough to start your own business, a positive relationship with a mentor or a friend who has successfully started their own business can provide you with the inspiration and motivation you need to challenge that belief and take action towards starting your own business.

Boosting Confidence and Self-Esteem

Confidence and self-esteem are essential components of a can-do attitude. When we believe in ourselves and our abilities, we are more likely to take risks and pursue our goals with determination and perseverance.

Positive relationships can help boost our confidence and self-esteem by providing us with the validation and recognition we need to feel good about ourselves. When we surround ourselves with people who appreciate us, value our contributions, and acknowledge our achievements, we are more likely to feel confident in our abilities and believe in ourselves.

On the other hand, negative relationships can have the opposite effect by undermining our confidence and self-esteem. When we are constantly criticized, belittled, or ignored, we are more likely to doubt ourselves and our abilities, which can lead to a negative attitude and a lack of motivation to pursue our goals.

Providing Support and Encouragement

Finally, positive relationships can provide us with the support and encouragement we need to achieve our goals. When we have a network of people who believe in us and want to see us succeed, we are more likely to stay motivated and push through the challenges we face.

Supportive relationships can come in many forms, such as a mentor who provides guidance and advice, a friend who listens and offers a shoulder to lean on, or a partner who shares our vision and supports us through thick and thin. Whatever form it takes, having positive relationships in our lives can make all the difference in our ability to cultivate a can-do attitude and achieve unprecedented success.

Conclusion

In conclusion, positive relationships are a vital component of cultivating a can-do attitude. They can help us overcome limiting beliefs, boost our confidence and self-esteem, and provide us with the support and encouragement we need to achieve our goals.

It's important to evaluate the relationships we have in our lives and determine which ones are positive and which ones are negative. By surrounding ourselves with people who believe in us, support us, and encourage us to pursue our dreams, we can develop a more positive mindset and cultivate a can-do attitude that will propel us towards unprecedented success in all areas of life.

However, it's also important to recognize that positive relationships require effort and maintenance. We need to be willing to invest time and energy into building and nurturing our relationships, and we need to be willing to give as much as we receive.

23: THE POWER OF POSITIVE RELATIONSHIPS IN A CAN-DO ATTITUDE

In summary, positive relationships are a powerful tool for cultivating a can-do attitude. By surrounding ourselves with people who believe in us, support us, and encourage us to pursue our goals, we can overcome limiting beliefs, boost our confidence and self-esteem, and achieve unprecedented success in all areas of life. So, let's make a conscious effort to build and nurture positive relationships, and unlock the true potential of a can-do attitude!

24: Cultivating a Growth Mindset with a Can-Do Attitude

Introduction:

Success is not just about talent or skills; it is also about attitude. Having a can-do attitude is an essential ingredient to achieve unprecedented success in all areas of life. A can-do attitude is a positive mindset that empowers individuals to embrace challenges, learn from failure, and persist in the face of obstacles. It is a mindset that fosters growth, creativity, and innovation. In this chapter, we will explore the concept of a growth mindset and how to cultivate it with a can-do attitude.

What is a Growth Mindset?

A growth mindset is a belief that individuals can develop their abilities through hard work, dedication, and persistence. According to Carol Dweck, a world-renowned Stanford psychologist, individuals with a growth mindset embrace challenges, learn from feedback, and persist in the face of obstacles. They see failures as opportunities to learn and grow, rather than evidence of their limitations. In contrast, individuals with a fixed mindset believe that their abilities are predetermined and cannot be changed. They tend to avoid challenges, give up easily, and view failures as a reflection of their incompetence.

The Benefits of a Growth Mindset:

Research has shown that a growth mindset is associated with numerous benefits, such as:

Increased resilience: Individuals with a growth mindset are more resilient in the face of challenges and setbacks. They view obstacles as opportunities to learn and grow, rather than as threats to their self-worth.

Improved performance: Individuals with a growth mindset are more likely to achieve their goals and reach their full potential. They are willing to put in the effort and persistence required to improve their skills and abilities.

Greater creativity: Individuals with a growth mindset are more open to new ideas and perspectives. They are more likely to experiment and take risks, which can lead to innovative solutions.

Enhanced well-being: Individuals with a growth mindset

are more likely to experience positive emotions, such as joy and fulfillment. They are less likely to experience negative emotions, such as anxiety and depression.

How to Cultivate a Growth Mindset with a Can-Do Attitude:

Cultivating a growth mindset requires a conscious effort to change our beliefs and attitudes. Here are some practical strategies to cultivate a growth mindset with a can-do attitude:

Embrace challenges: Instead of avoiding challenges, embrace them as opportunities to learn and grow. Seek out challenges that push you out of your comfort zone and allow you to develop new skills and abilities.

Learn from feedback: Instead of ignoring or resisting feedback, use it as a tool for growth and improvement. Ask for feedback from trusted sources and use it to identify areas for improvement.

Persist in the face of obstacles: Instead of giving up when faced with obstacles, persist and find new ways to overcome them. Use setbacks as opportunities to learn and adapt your approach.

Adopt a can-do attitude: Instead of focusing on limitations, adopt a can-do attitude that empowers you to believe in your abilities and take action towards your goals. Focus on what you can do, rather than what you cannot do.

Surround yourself with positive influences: Surround yourself with people who inspire and support your growth mindset. Seek out mentors, coaches, and peers who embody a can-do attitude and encourage you to pursue your goals.

Conclusion:

Cultivating a growth mindset with a can-do attitude is a powerful tool to achieve unprecedented success in all areas of life. By embracing challenges, learning from feedback, persisting in the face of obstacles, adopting a can-do attitude, and surrounding yourself with positive influences, you can transform your mindset and unlock your true potential. Remember, success is not just about talent or skills; it is also about attitude. With a growth mindset and a can-do attitude, you can achieve anything you set your mind to.

25: Overcoming Procrastination and Taking Action with a Can-Do Attitude

Introduction

Procrastination is one of the biggest obstacles to success. It is the habit of putting off important tasks and instead choosing to do something less important or enjoyable. Everyone has procrastinated at some point in their lives, but if it becomes a habit, it can lead to serious consequences such as missed deadlines, lost opportunities, and unfulfilled potential.

In this chapter, we will explore the reasons behind procrastination, the negative effects it can have on our lives, and most importantly, how to overcome it with a can-do attitude. We will provide practical tips and strategies to help you take action and achieve your goals.

Understanding Procrastination

Procrastination is often misunderstood as laziness or lack of motivation. However, the root cause of procrastination is usually fear – fear of failure, fear of success, fear of criticism, or fear of the unknown. When we feel overwhelmed or uncertain about a task, our brains instinctively seek comfort and pleasure in activities that are easier and more familiar, such as checking social media or watching TV.

The problem with procrastination is that it provides temporary relief but leads to long-term pain. By avoiding important tasks, we create more stress and anxiety for ourselves, which in turn reinforces the habit of procrastination. Procrastination also robs us of the sense of accomplishment and satisfaction that comes with completing a task and achieving a goal.

Negative Effects of Procrastination

Procrastination can have serious negative effects on our personal and professional lives. Here are some examples:

Missed deadlines: Procrastination can lead to missed deadlines, which can have serious consequences in the workplace, school, or personal projects. Missing a deadline can damage your reputation, lead to financial losses, or even cause harm to others in some cases.

25: OVERCOMING PROCRASTINATION AND TAKING ACTION WITH A CAN-DO ATTITUDE

Reduced productivity: Procrastination can reduce productivity and efficiency, as it often involves spending more time and energy on unimportant tasks rather than the most important ones.

Health problems: Procrastination can also have negative effects on your physical and mental health. It can increase stress, anxiety, and depression, and lead to poor sleep, low energy, and a weakened immune system.

Missed opportunities: Procrastination can prevent you from taking advantage of opportunities that come your way, whether it's a job offer, a chance to travel, or a new hobby.

Overcoming Procrastination with a Can-Do Attitude

Overcoming procrastination is not easy, but it is possible with a can-do attitude. A can-do attitude is the belief that you can accomplish anything you set your mind to, regardless of the obstacles or challenges you may face. Here are some practical tips to help you develop a can-do attitude and overcome procrastination:

Set clear goals: Setting clear, specific goals is the first step in overcoming procrastination. When you have a clear idea of what you want to achieve, it becomes easier to focus your energy and attention on the most important tasks. Write down your goals and break them down into smaller, manageable steps.

Visualize success: Visualization is a powerful tool for overcoming procrastination. Close your eyes and imagine yourself completing the task successfully, feeling proud of yourself, and enjoying the rewards of your hard work. This can help you overcome the fear and uncertainty that often underlies procrastination.

Eliminate distractions: Distractions are one of the biggest obstacles to productivity and can fuel procrastination. Identify the sources of distraction in your environment and take steps to eliminate or minimize them. This might mean turning off your phone, closing your email, or finding a quiet place to work.

Use the Pomodoro Technique: The Pomodoro Technique is a time-management method that involves working for a set amount of time (usually 25 minutes) and then taking a short break (usually 5 minutes) before starting the next work session. This technique can help you stay focused and avoid distractions, as well as break down large tasks into smaller, more manageable chunks.

Practice self-compassion: Procrastination often leads to feelings of guilt, shame, and self-criticism, which can make the problem worse. Instead of beating yourself up for procrastinating, practice self-compassion and treat yourself with kindness and understanding. Remember that procrastination is a common problem that can be overcome with time and effort.

Use positive self-talk: Positive self-talk is another powerful tool for overcoming procrastination. Instead of telling yourself that you can't do something or that it's too hard, use positive affirmations to boost your confidence and motivation. For example, tell yourself "I can do this" or "I am capable and competent."

Break the cycle of perfectionism: Perfectionism can fuel procrastination by creating unrealistic expectations and a fear of failure. Instead of striving for perfection, focus on progress and improvement. Accept that mistakes are part of the learning process and that it's okay to make them.

25: OVERCOMING PROCRASTINATION AND TAKING ACTION WITH A CAN-DO ATTITUDE

Use accountability: Accountability can be a powerful motivator for overcoming procrastination. Tell a friend, family member, or colleague about your goals and ask them to hold you accountable. This can help you stay on track and avoid the temptation to procrastinate.

Reward yourself: Rewards can be a powerful motivator for taking action and overcoming procrastination. Set up a reward system for yourself, such as treating yourself to your favorite food or activity after completing a task or reaching a milestone.

Conclusion

Procrastination is a common problem that can have serious negative effects on our personal and professional lives. However, it is possible to overcome procrastination with a can-do attitude. By setting clear goals, visualizing success, eliminating distractions, using the Pomodoro Technique, practicing self-compassion and positive self-talk, breaking the cycle of perfectionism, using accountability, and rewarding yourself, you can take action and achieve your goals. Remember that overcoming procrastination is a process that takes time and effort, but with a can-do attitude, anything is possible!

26: The Importance of Accountability in a Can-Do Attitude

In life, there are many factors that contribute to success. Hard work, perseverance, determination, and talent are all important, but there is one quality that is often overlooked: accountability. A can-do attitude requires taking responsibility for one's actions, and being accountable for one's decisions, both good and bad. In this chapter, we will explore the importance of accountability in cultivating a can-do attitude, and how to develop this quality in yourself.

The Power of Accountability

Accountability is the cornerstone of personal and professional growth. It is the ability to take ownership of your actions and decisions, and to accept the consequences that come with them. Being accountable means that you are willing to acknowledge your mistakes, learn from them, and take steps to prevent them from happening again. This quality is essential for success in all areas of life, from relationships to career.

When you are accountable for your actions, you become more reliable and trustworthy. People are more likely to respect and trust you when they know that you will follow through on your commitments and take responsibility for any mistakes or failures. In a professional setting, accountability can lead to promotions and increased opportunities, as employers value employees who are accountable and take initiative.

Accountability also plays a crucial role in personal growth. When you take responsibility for your mistakes, you are able to learn from them and grow as a person. This self-reflection allows you to identify your strengths and weaknesses, and to make positive changes in your life. It also helps you to build self-esteem, as you take pride in your accomplishments and take ownership of your failures.

Developing Accountability

If you struggle with being accountable, there are steps you can take to develop this quality in yourself. Here are some tips to help you become more accountable:

Take ownership of your actions: Start by acknowledging your mistakes and taking responsibility for them. Avoid making excuses or blaming others for your failures. Instead, focus on what you can do to fix the situation and prevent it from happening again.

Set clear goals: When you set clear goals for yourself, you are more likely to hold yourself accountable for achieving them. Write down your goals and create a plan for how you will achieve them. Track your progress and hold yourself accountable for meeting your milestones.

Seek feedback: Ask for feedback from others on your performance and behavior. This will help you to identify areas where you can improve and hold yourself accountable for making those changes.

Build a support system: Surround yourself with people who will hold you accountable and support you in your goals. This can be a mentor, coach, or accountability partner.

Learn from your mistakes: When you make a mistake, take the time to reflect on what went wrong and what you could have done differently. Use this knowledge to make positive changes in your behavior and decision-making.

Accountability in a Can-Do Attitude

26: THE IMPORTANCE OF ACCOUNTABILITY IN A CAN-DO ATTITUDE

Accountability is a key component of a can-do attitude. When you have a can-do attitude, you approach challenges with a positive and proactive mindset. You believe that you can overcome obstacles and achieve your goals, but you also recognize that success requires hard work and personal responsibility.

A can-do attitude requires taking ownership of your actions and decisions, and being accountable for the results. It means being willing to take risks and try new things, but also being willing to learn from your failures and make changes as needed. It is a mindset that values progress over perfection, and embraces challenges as opportunities for growth.

In order to cultivate a can-do attitude, it is important to develop a strong sense of accountability. This means taking responsibility for your actions, setting clear goals, seeking feedback, building a support system, and learning from your mistakes. When you are accountable for your actions, you are better able to achieve your goals and overcome challenges with a positive and determined attitude.

Accountability also helps you to build trust and credibility with others. When you are known for being accountable and reliable, people are more likely to want to work with you and support you in your endeavors. This can lead to increased opportunities for growth and success in both your personal and professional life.

Another benefit of accountability is that it helps you to stay focused on your goals. When you are accountable for your actions, you are more likely to stay committed to achieving your goals, even when faced with challenges or setbacks. You are less likely to give up or become discouraged, because you know that you are responsible for your own success.

In addition, accountability can also help you to develop resilience and perseverance. When you take ownership of your mistakes and failures, you are able to learn from them and make positive changes. This helps you to bounce back stronger and more determined than ever before, and to continue striving towards your goals despite any obstacles that may come your way.

Conclusion

26: THE IMPORTANCE OF ACCOUNTABILITY IN A CAN-DO ATTITUDE

In conclusion, accountability is a critical component of a can-do attitude. It is the ability to take ownership of your actions and decisions, and to accept the consequences that come with them. When you are accountable, you become more reliable and trustworthy, and you are better able to achieve your goals and overcome challenges with a positive and determined attitude.

If you struggle with being accountable, there are steps you can take to develop this quality in yourself. Start by taking ownership of your actions, setting clear goals, seeking feedback, building a support system, and learning from your mistakes. With practice, you can cultivate a can-do attitude that will help you to achieve unprecedented success in all areas of your life.

27: The Connection between a Can-Do Attitude and Creativity

Introduction

A can-do attitude is essential for success in all areas of life. It is a positive mindset that helps you to overcome obstacles and achieve your goals. One of the key benefits of having a can-do attitude is that it allows you to be more creative. In this chapter, we will explore the connection between a can-do attitude and creativity. We will look at how a can-do attitude can help you to unlock your creativity, overcome creative blocks, and achieve unprecedented success in all areas of life.

What is Creativity?

Creativity is the ability to come up with new and innovative ideas, solutions, and approaches to problems. It is a vital skill that is essential for success in all areas of life, from business and entrepreneurship to art and design. Creativity is not something that is limited to a select few; it is a skill that can be developed and cultivated over time. Creativity involves being open-minded, curious, and willing to take risks.

27: THE CONNECTION BETWEEN A CAN-DO ATTITUDE AND CREATIVITY

The Connection between a Can-Do Attitude and Creativity

A can-do attitude is a positive mindset that is characterized by optimism, resilience, and a belief in oneself. It is the attitude that says "I can do this" rather than "this is too hard" or "I can't do this." A can-do attitude is essential for creativity because it allows you to approach challenges with a sense of possibility and curiosity rather than fear and doubt.

When you have a can-do attitude, you are more likely to take risks and try new things. This willingness to experiment and take risks is essential for creativity because it allows you to explore new ideas and approaches. Creativity often involves stepping outside of your comfort zone and taking risks, and a can-do attitude makes this easier.

Another way in which a can-do attitude can boost creativity is by helping you to overcome creative blocks. Creative blocks are the barriers that prevent you from coming up with new ideas or solutions. They can be caused by fear, self-doubt, or a lack of inspiration. When you have a can-do attitude, you are better equipped to overcome these blocks because you approach them with a sense of optimism and determination.

27: THE CONNECTION BETWEEN A CAN-DO ATTITUDE AND CREATIVITY

A can-do attitude can also help you to cultivate a growth mindset. A growth mindset is the belief that your abilities and intelligence can be developed over time through hard work and dedication. When you have a growth mindset, you are more likely to embrace challenges and see them as opportunities for growth and learning. This mindset is essential for creativity because it allows you to approach problems with a sense of curiosity and a willingness to learn.

Practical Tips for Cultivating a Can-Do Attitude and Boosting Creativity

Now that we have established the connection between a can-do attitude and creativity, let's explore some practical tips for cultivating a can-do attitude and boosting your creativity.

Believe in Yourself

The first step in cultivating a can-do attitude is to believe in yourself. This means recognizing your strengths and abilities and having confidence in your ability to overcome challenges. One way to do this is to create a list of your achievements and accomplishments. This can help you to see that you are capable of achieving great things.

Embrace Failure

Failure is an inevitable part of the creative process. Rather than seeing failure as a negative thing, try to embrace it as an opportunity for growth and learning. When you encounter a setback or a failure, ask yourself what you can learn from the experience and how you can use it to improve your approach.

Take Risks

As we have already mentioned, taking risks is essential for creativity. When you have a can-do attitude, you are more likely to take risks and try new things. This could involve experimenting with a new idea, trying a new approach, or stepping outside of your comfort zone.

Surround Yourself with Positive and Supportive People

The people you surround yourself with can have a significant impact on your mindset and your ability to be creative. Surround yourself with positive and supportive people who believe in your abilities and encourage you to take risks and try new things. Avoid negative and toxic people who bring you down and discourage you from pursuing your dreams.

Practice Mindfulness

Mindfulness is the practice of being present and fully engaged in the moment. It can help you to reduce stress and anxiety, which can be major barriers to creativity. Try practicing mindfulness through activities such as meditation, yoga, or simply taking a few deep breaths and focusing on the present moment.

Stay Inspired

Creativity requires inspiration, so it's important to find ways to stay inspired and motivated. This could involve reading books, attending workshops or conferences, listening to podcasts or TED talks, or simply taking a walk in nature. Find what inspires you and make time for it in your life.

Keep Learning and Growing

Finally, it's important to keep learning and growing if you want to cultivate a can-do attitude and be more creative.

27: THE CONNECTION BETWEEN A CAN-DO ATTITUDE AND CREATIVITY

This could involve taking courses or workshops, reading books or articles, or simply seeking out new experiences and challenges. Keep an open mind and be willing to learn and grow in all areas of your life.

Conclusion

In conclusion, a can-do attitude is essential for creativity and success in all areas of life. By cultivating a positive mindset, embracing failure, taking risks, surrounding yourself with positive and supportive people, practicing mindfulness, staying inspired, and continuing to learn and grow, you can unlock your creativity and achieve unprecedented success. Remember that creativity is not limited to a select few; it is a skill that can be developed and cultivated over time. With a can-do attitude and a willingness to learn and grow, you can become a more creative and successful person in all areas of your life.

28: Taking Risks and Trying New Things with a Can-Do Attitude

Do you find yourself stuck in a rut, doing the same things day in and day out? Do you feel like you're not living up to your full potential, and that there's more to life than what you're currently experiencing? If so, you're not alone. Many people feel this way, but few take the steps necessary to change their circumstances.

The truth is, success and fulfillment come to those who are willing to take risks and try new things. It's easy to get comfortable in our routines and stick to what we know, but that kind of complacency can lead to stagnation and a lack of growth. In this chapter, we'll explore the importance of taking risks and trying new things with a can-do attitude, and how doing so can unlock your true potential and lead to unprecedented success in all areas of your life.

Taking risks is an essential part of personal and professional growth. Without risk, there can be no reward. Whether you're starting a new business, pursuing a new hobby, or taking on a new role at work, there will always be an element of risk involved. But it's through taking those risks that we learn and grow.

28: TAKING RISKS AND TRYING NEW THINGS WITH A CAN-DO ATTITUDE

When we take risks, we're forced to step outside of our comfort zones and face our fears. We're forced to confront the unknown and embrace uncertainty. This can be scary, but it's also exhilarating. When we push ourselves beyond what we thought was possible, we discover new strengths and abilities we didn't know we had.

One of the main reasons people hesitate to take risks is because of limiting beliefs. Limiting beliefs are the stories we tell ourselves about what we're capable of and what's possible. These beliefs are often rooted in fear and can hold us back from achieving our true potential.

To overcome limiting beliefs, we must first recognize them. What are the stories you tell yourself about your abilities and what's possible for you? Are these beliefs serving you, or are they holding you back?

Once you've identified your limiting beliefs, it's important to challenge them. Ask yourself, "Is this belief really true? What evidence do I have to support it?" Often, we find that our limiting beliefs are based on false assumptions or outdated information.

28: TAKING RISKS AND TRYING NEW THINGS WITH A CAN-DO ATTITUDE

Finally, replace your limiting beliefs with empowering beliefs. Instead of telling yourself you're not good enough or not capable of success, tell yourself that you can do anything you set your mind to. Believe in yourself and your abilities, and you'll be amazed at what you can accomplish.

Another reason people avoid taking risks is because they're afraid of failure. But failure is not something to be feared. In fact, failure is an essential part of the learning process. When we fail, we're forced to examine our mistakes and figure out what went wrong. This process helps us grow and improve.

The key to embracing failure is to view it as an opportunity for growth, rather than a personal defeat. When we fail, we should ask ourselves, "What did I learn from this experience? How can I improve next time?" By reframing failure as a learning opportunity, we can turn it into a positive experience.

Trying new things has many benefits beyond personal growth. When we try new things, we open ourselves up to new experiences and opportunities. We expand our knowledge and understanding of the world around us. We become more adaptable and resilient, able to handle whatever challenges come our way.

Trying new things can also be a great way to discover new passions and hobbies. You never know what you might enjoy until you give it a try. By exploring new activities and interests, we can find new sources of joy and fulfillment in our lives.

Furthermore, trying new things can help us build stronger relationships with others. When we share new experiences with friends and family, we create memories that deepen our bonds with one another. Trying new things can also be a great way to meet new people and expand our social circles.

To truly embrace the power of taking risks and trying new things, we need to cultivate a can-do attitude. A can-do attitude is a mindset that embraces challenges and sees opportunities in every situation. It's an attitude of optimism and perseverance that empowers us to overcome obstacles and achieve our goals.

Cultivating a can-do attitude starts with a willingness to take risks and try new things. We need to be willing to step outside of our comfort zones and embrace uncertainty. We need to be willing to face our fears and push ourselves beyond what we thought was possible.

But cultivating a can-do attitude also requires a commitment to growth and learning. We need to be open to feedback and willing to make changes when necessary. We need to be willing to learn from our mistakes and keep pushing ourselves to improve.

If you're ready to start taking risks and trying new things with a can-do attitude, here are some practical tips to get you started:

– Start small. You don't have to take a huge risk right away. Start with something small and build from there.

– Set goals. Identify what you want to achieve and create a plan for how to get there.

– Get support. Surround yourself with people who encourage and support you.

– Embrace failure. Remember that failure is an essential part of the learning process.

28: TAKING RISKS AND TRYING NEW THINGS WITH A CAN-DO ATTITUDE

– Celebrate your successes. Take time to acknowledge and celebrate your accomplishments.

– Keep learning. Continuously seek out new knowledge and experiences to help you grow.

– Stay positive. Focus on the opportunities, not the obstacles.

Taking risks and trying new things with a can-do attitude is essential for personal and professional growth. When we push ourselves beyond what we thought was possible, we discover new strengths and abilities we didn't know we had. We become more adaptable and resilient, able to handle whatever challenges come our way.

To cultivate a can-do attitude, we need to be willing to take risks, challenge our limiting beliefs, and embrace failure as an opportunity for growth. By doing so, we can unlock our true potential and achieve unprecedented success in all areas of our lives. So, what are you waiting for? Embrace the power of a can-do attitude and start taking risks and trying new things today!

29: The Role of Self-Discipline in a Can-Do Attitude

Introduction

Self-discipline is one of the most crucial components of a can-do attitude. It is the foundation on which we build the habits and routines that drive us towards our goals. Without self-discipline, we are at the mercy of our impulses, emotions, and distractions, and we may find ourselves constantly struggling to stay focused and motivated.

In this chapter, we will explore the role of self-discipline in a can-do attitude, and why it is essential for achieving unprecedented success in all areas of life. We will discuss how self-discipline works, how to cultivate it, and how to overcome the obstacles that may stand in our way.

The Power of Self-Discipline

Self-discipline is the ability to control one's impulses, emotions, and behavior in pursuit of a goal. It is the ability to delay gratification, resist temptation, and persevere through adversity. Self-discipline is not a trait that we are born with; it is a skill that we can develop through practice and repetition.

The power of self-discipline lies in its ability to create habits and routines that lead to success. When we have the discipline to follow a set of habits consistently, we develop a sense of mastery and control over our lives. We become more productive, efficient, and focused on our goals, and we are less likely to be derailed by distractions and setbacks.

Self-discipline also enables us to overcome our limiting beliefs and self-doubt. When we have the discipline to work towards our goals, we build a sense of self-efficacy and confidence in our abilities. We begin to believe that we can achieve anything we set our minds to, and we are more likely to take risks and pursue ambitious goals.

Cultivating Self-Discipline

Cultivating self-discipline requires a conscious effort to change our habits and behaviors. It requires us to be honest with ourselves about our weaknesses and shortcomings, and to take deliberate steps to overcome them.

One of the most effective ways to cultivate self-discipline is to start small. We can begin by setting small goals that are easy to achieve and gradually increase their difficulty over time. For example, if we want to develop the habit of regular exercise, we can start by committing to a short walk every day and gradually increase the duration and intensity of our workouts.

Another effective way to cultivate self-discipline is to establish a routine. By creating a set of habits that we follow consistently, we develop a sense of structure and predictability in our lives. This can help us to stay focused on our goals and avoid distractions.

It is also important to eliminate sources of temptation and distraction. We can do this by removing any objects or activities that may distract us from our goals. For example, if we want to spend more time reading, we may need to turn off our phone or computer to avoid distractions.

Overcoming Obstacles

Despite our best efforts, there will be times when we struggle to maintain our self-discipline. We may face setbacks, distractions, or obstacles that make it difficult to stay focused on our goals. However, it is important to remember that setbacks and failures are a natural part of the learning process, and we should not let them discourage us.

One of the best ways to overcome obstacles is to develop a growth mindset. A growth mindset is the belief that our abilities and intelligence can be developed through hard work and dedication. When we have a growth mindset, we are more likely to see obstacles as opportunities for learning and growth, rather than as insurmountable challenges.

Another effective way to overcome obstacles is to seek support from others. We can seek guidance and advice from mentors, coaches, or friends who have faced similar challenges. We can also build a network of support by joining a community of like-minded individuals who share our goals and values.

It is also important to practice self-compassion and avoid self-criticism. When we experience setbacks or failures, it can be easy to become discouraged and blame ourselves. However, self-criticism can be counterproductive and may even sabotage our efforts to achieve our goals. Instead, we should practice self-compassion and remind ourselves that setbacks are a natural part of the learning process.

Conclusion

In conclusion, self-discipline is a crucial component of a can-do attitude. It enables us to develop the habits and routines that lead to success, and to overcome our limiting beliefs and self-doubt. Cultivating self-discipline requires a conscious effort to change our habits and behaviors, and to overcome the obstacles that may stand in our way. However, with practice and persistence, we can develop the self-discipline we need to achieve unprecedented success in all areas of life.

30: The Importance of Continuous Learning with a Can-Do Attitude

Introduction

Success in any aspect of life requires continuous learning and improvement. Without continuous learning, we risk becoming stagnant and complacent, limiting our potential for growth and achievement. A can-do attitude is all about pushing past limitations and believing that we can achieve our goals, no matter how big or small. This chapter will explore the importance of continuous learning with a can-do attitude, and how it can help us to unlock our true potential and achieve unprecedented success.

The Benefits of Continuous Learning

Continuous learning is the process of gaining knowledge, skills, and experiences throughout our lives. It involves actively seeking out new information, challenges, and opportunities to grow and improve. There are many benefits to continuous learning, including:

Personal Growth: Continuous learning allows us to broaden

our perspectives, challenge our beliefs, and expand our knowledge and skills. This can lead to personal growth and development, as we become more self-aware and better equipped to navigate life's challenges.

Career Advancement: In today's rapidly changing job market, continuous learning is essential for career advancement. By developing new skills and staying up-to-date with industry trends, we can increase our value as employees and position ourselves for new opportunities.

Improved Confidence: Learning new things can boost our confidence and self-esteem, as we gain a sense of mastery and accomplishment. This can help us to overcome fears and self-doubt, and approach challenges with a can-do attitude.

Better Health: Continuous learning has been linked to improved cognitive function and brain health. It can also help us to reduce stress and improve our overall well-being, as we engage in activities that are meaningful and fulfilling.

Cultivating a Can-Do Attitude through Continuous Learning

30: THE IMPORTANCE OF CONTINUOUS LEARNING WITH A CAN-DO ATTITUDE

A can-do attitude is all about believing in our ability to overcome obstacles and achieve our goals. Continuous learning is a key component of cultivating this mindset, as it helps us to build confidence, develop new skills, and expand our knowledge and understanding of the world.

Here are some ways that we can cultivate a can-do attitude through continuous learning:

Set Learning Goals: Identify areas where you would like to grow and develop, and set specific learning goals for yourself. This could include taking a course, reading a book, or attending a workshop or seminar. By setting goals, you give yourself something to work towards, and a sense of accomplishment when you achieve them.

Embrace Challenges: Embrace new challenges and opportunities to learn, even if they feel uncomfortable or intimidating. This can help you to push past your limitations and develop a can-do attitude. Remember, every challenge is an opportunity to learn and grow.

Seek Feedback: Seek feedback from others to help you identify areas where you can improve. This can be difficult at first, but it can be a powerful tool for growth and development. Remember, feedback is not criticism - it is an opportunity to learn and improve.

Reflect on Your Learning: Take time to reflect on your learning and identify what you have gained from the experience. This can help you to internalize what you have learned and apply it in your life.

Conclusion

Continuous learning is essential for personal and professional growth, and it is a key component of a can-do attitude. By embracing new challenges and opportunities to learn, we can develop the skills, knowledge, and confidence to achieve our goals and unlock our true potential. Remember, a can-do attitude is not about being perfect or never making mistakes - it is about believing in yourself and your ability to overcome obstacles and achieve your dreams.

31: Overcoming Imposter Syndrome with a Can-Do Attitude

Imposter syndrome is a phenomenon that affects many people, regardless of their background, profession, or achievements. It is a condition where an individual doubts their abilities and accomplishments and feels like a fraud. Even the most successful and accomplished individuals can fall victim to imposter syndrome, leading to anxiety, low self-esteem, and decreased confidence. However, with a can-do attitude, it is possible to overcome imposter syndrome and achieve unprecedented success in all areas of life.

To understand how to overcome imposter syndrome with a can-do attitude, it is essential to first understand what imposter syndrome is and its causes. Imposter syndrome is a psychological phenomenon where individuals doubt their abilities and accomplishments and feel like they do not deserve their success. These individuals believe that they have only succeeded due to luck, timing, or external factors and not because of their talent, skills, or hard work.

The causes of imposter syndrome are complex and multifaceted. They can be influenced by a person's upbringing, experiences, and personality traits. For instance, individuals who were raised in highly critical or competitive environments may be more susceptible to imposter syndrome. Similarly, people with perfectionist tendencies or high-achievers may feel like they have not achieved enough, even if they have accomplished significant success.

To overcome imposter syndrome, it is necessary to cultivate a can-do attitude. A can-do attitude is a mindset of optimism, resilience, and determination that empowers individuals to believe in their abilities, take risks, and overcome obstacles. A can-do attitude involves embracing challenges, seeking opportunities for growth, and believing in oneself.

The first step to developing a can-do attitude is to identify and challenge limiting beliefs. Limiting beliefs are thoughts and beliefs that hold individuals back from achieving their goals and reaching their full potential. These beliefs can be deeply ingrained and may be difficult to recognize. However, by becoming aware of them, it is possible to challenge and reframe them to more empowering beliefs.

For instance, instead of believing that success is due to external factors, such as luck or timing, individuals can reframe their belief to recognize their talent, skills, and hard work. Additionally, instead of focusing on their flaws and mistakes, individuals can embrace them as opportunities for growth and improvement.

The second step to developing a can-do attitude is to take action towards one's goals. Action is a crucial component of success, and individuals with a can-do attitude are not afraid to take risks, fail, and learn from their mistakes. They view failure as a necessary part of the journey towards success and use setbacks as motivation to keep moving forward.

Taking action can also involve seeking out opportunities for growth and learning. Individuals with a can-do attitude are not afraid to step outside their comfort zones, take on new challenges, and learn new skills. They recognize that every experience, even the ones that do not go as planned, can be a valuable learning opportunity.

The third step to developing a can-do attitude is to cultivate a supportive network. Having a supportive network of friends, family, mentors, and peers can provide individuals with the encouragement, guidance, and feedback necessary to achieve success. It is essential to surround oneself with individuals who believe in one's abilities and are willing to support and challenge them to reach their full potential.

Lastly, it is crucial to celebrate one's accomplishments and successes. Individuals with imposter syndrome often downplay their achievements or dismiss them as insignificant. However, celebrating one's accomplishments can reinforce the belief in one's abilities and provide motivation to continue striving towards one's goals.

In conclusion, imposter syndrome is a prevalent phenomenon that can hinder individuals' success and happiness. However, with a can-do attitude, it is possible to overcome imposter syndrome and achieve unprecedented success in all areas of life. Developing a can-do attitude involves challenging limiting beliefs, taking action towards one's goals, seeking out opportunities for growth and learning, cultivating a supportive network, and celebrating one's accomplishments. By cultivating a can-do attitude, individuals can empower themselves to believe in their abilities, take risks, and overcome obstacles to achieve their goals.

It is essential to recognize that developing a can-do attitude is not a one-time process but rather an ongoing journey. It involves continuous self-reflection, self-awareness, and growth. It is essential to be patient and kind to oneself and recognize that setbacks and failures are a natural part of the journey towards success.

One effective way to cultivate a can-do attitude is through mindfulness practices. Mindfulness involves being present and aware of one's thoughts, feelings, and surroundings without judgment. Mindfulness can help individuals recognize and challenge limiting beliefs, overcome negative self-talk, and increase self-awareness and self-compassion.

Another effective way to cultivate a can-do attitude is through goal-setting. Setting goals can provide individuals with direction, motivation, and a sense of purpose. It is essential to set realistic and achievable goals, break them down into smaller, manageable steps, and celebrate progress along the way.

Finally, it is essential to seek help from professionals if imposter syndrome or other mental health concerns are impacting one's daily life. Seeking help from a mental health professional can provide individuals with tools, support, and guidance to overcome imposter syndrome and achieve their goals.

In conclusion, imposter syndrome can be a significant obstacle to achieving success and happiness. However, by cultivating a can-do attitude, individuals can empower themselves to believe in their abilities, take risks, and overcome obstacles. Developing a can-do attitude involves challenging limiting beliefs, taking action towards one's goals, seeking out opportunities for growth and learning, cultivating a supportive network, and celebrating one's accomplishments. By taking these steps and seeking help when necessary, individuals can overcome imposter syndrome and achieve unprecedented success in all areas of life.

32: The Role of Intuition in a Can-Do Attitude

Intuition is a powerful tool that can help you make better decisions and navigate through life's challenges with confidence. It's a gut feeling or a hunch that guides you towards the right path, even when you don't have all the facts or data at hand. In this chapter, we'll explore the role of intuition in developing a can-do attitude and how you can tap into your intuitive wisdom to unlock your true potential.

Intuition is often misunderstood as a mystical or supernatural ability, but it's actually a natural ability that we all possess. It's a form of intelligence that operates beyond the rational mind, and it's closely linked to our emotions and bodily sensations. Intuition is like a compass that guides us towards our true north, even when the terrain is unfamiliar or challenging.

Having a can-do attitude means being open to new experiences and possibilities, and trusting yourself to handle whatever comes your way. It means being willing to take risks and face your fears, knowing that you have the inner resources to overcome any obstacle. Intuition plays a key role in developing this mindset because it helps you tune into your inner wisdom and navigate through uncertainty with confidence.

One of the challenges of developing intuition is learning to distinguish it from other forms of mental noise, such as fear, anxiety, or wishful thinking. When you're facing a decision or a problem, your mind may be filled with all sorts of thoughts and emotions, and it can be hard to know which ones are coming from your intuition and which ones are just noise.

One way to cultivate your intuition is to practice mindfulness and self-awareness. This means taking time to tune into your body and your emotions, and noticing how they change in response to different situations. You can also try meditation, yoga, or other practices that help you quiet your mind and connect with your inner wisdom.

Another way to develop your intuition is to pay attention to your dreams and the symbols and images that come up in them. Your dreams can be a rich source of guidance and insight, and they often reflect your subconscious desires and fears. By keeping a dream journal and reflecting on your dreams, you can gain a deeper understanding of your inner world and tap into your intuition.

It's also important to trust your intuition and act on it, even when it goes against your rational mind or the opinions of others. Your intuition may lead you to take risks or make unconventional choices, but these are often the very things that lead to breakthroughs and successes. By following your intuition, you're tapping into your true potential and living from a place of authenticity and courage.

Of course, developing intuition is not a one-time event but an ongoing process. It requires practice, patience, and a willingness to embrace uncertainty and the unknown. But with time and effort, you can learn to trust your inner guidance and cultivate a can-do attitude that empowers you to achieve unprecedented success in all areas of your life.

In conclusion, intuition is a powerful tool that can help you unlock your true potential and develop a can-do attitude that leads to success and fulfillment. By cultivating mindfulness, self-awareness, and trust in your intuition, you can tap into your inner wisdom and navigate through life's challenges with confidence and grace. So, go ahead and listen to that inner voice that's urging you to take a bold step or try something new – it just might be the key to unlocking your true potential!

33: Using a Can-Do Attitude to Overcome Obstacles and Challenges

Obstacles and challenges are an inevitable part of life. No matter how much we try to plan and prepare, life has a way of throwing curveballs at us. However, it is not the obstacle itself that defines us, but how we react to it. With a can-do attitude, we can transform our mindset and tackle any obstacle that comes our way.

So, what is a can-do attitude? A can-do attitude is a mindset that believes in one's ability to achieve and overcome any challenge. It is a positive, proactive, and solution-oriented approach to life. With a can-do attitude, obstacles and challenges are seen as opportunities for growth and development, rather than insurmountable barriers.

The first step to cultivating a can-do attitude is to identify and overcome limiting beliefs. Limiting beliefs are the negative thoughts and beliefs we hold about ourselves, others, and the world around us. They are the stories we tell ourselves that keep us stuck and prevent us from achieving our full potential.

33: USING A CAN-DO ATTITUDE TO OVERCOME OBSTACLES AND CHALLENGES

To overcome limiting beliefs, we must first become aware of them. We need to identify the negative self-talk that goes on in our heads and challenge it. We must ask ourselves, "Is this belief true? Is there evidence to support it? How is it holding me back?" By questioning our limiting beliefs, we can start to see them for what they are – stories we tell ourselves that are not necessarily true.

Once we have identified our limiting beliefs, we can start to replace them with positive, empowering beliefs. For example, instead of saying, "I'm not good enough," we can say, "I am capable and competent." Instead of saying, "I'll never be successful," we can say, "I have the skills and determination to achieve my goals." By replacing limiting beliefs with positive affirmations, we can start to shift our mindset and develop a can-do attitude.

The next step to cultivating a can-do attitude is to focus on solutions, not problems. When faced with an obstacle or challenge, it is easy to get bogged down in the problem itself. However, a can-do attitude focuses on finding solutions, not dwelling on problems. We must ask ourselves, "What can I do to overcome this obstacle? What resources do I have? Who can I reach out to for help?" By focusing on solutions, we can start to see a way forward and take action.

Another key component of a can-do attitude is perseverance. Perseverance is the ability to keep going even when things get tough. It is the determination to overcome obstacles and achieve our goals, no matter what. With a can-do attitude, we see setbacks as temporary and use them as motivation to keep pushing forward.

To cultivate perseverance, we must first set clear goals and develop a plan of action. We must break down our goals into smaller, manageable tasks and focus on one step at a time. We must also be willing to adapt and make changes along the way. Sometimes, the path to success is not a straight line, and we may need to pivot or try a different approach.

Finally, a can-do attitude is about embracing challenges and stepping outside our comfort zone. It is about taking risks and trying new things, even if they are scary or unfamiliar. With a can-do attitude, we see challenges as opportunities for growth and development. We embrace the unknown and use it as a chance to learn and expand our horizons.

33: USING A CAN-DO ATTITUDE TO OVERCOME OBSTACLES AND CHALLENGES

To embrace challenges, we must first identify our comfort zone and the areas where we tend to play it safe. We need to challenge ourselves to try new things and take risks, even if they are small at first. We can start by trying a new hobby, speaking up in a meeting, or reaching out to someone new. By stepping outside our comfort zone, we can start to build confidence and expand our abilities.

It's important to remember that developing a can-do attitude is a process, and it takes time and effort. But with consistent practice and the right mindset, we can overcome obstacles and achieve our goals.

One way to practice a can-do attitude is to reframe our language and focus on positive self-talk. Instead of saying, "I can't do this," we can say, "I haven't figured out how to do this yet." Instead of saying, "This is too hard," we can say, "This is challenging, but I can overcome it." By reframing our language, we can start to shift our mindset and develop a can-do attitude.

Another way to practice a can-do attitude is to seek out inspiration and motivation from others. We can surround ourselves with people who have a can-do attitude and who inspire us to be our best selves. We can read books, listen to podcasts, or attend events that promote a positive, proactive mindset. By immersing ourselves in a can-do culture, we can start to internalize this mindset and make it our own.

In addition, it's important to take care of our physical and mental health. A healthy body and mind are essential for cultivating a can-do attitude. We can exercise regularly, eat a balanced diet, and practice mindfulness and self-care. By taking care of ourselves, we can increase our energy, focus, and resilience, which are all essential for overcoming obstacles and achieving our goals.

Finally, we must remember that setbacks and failures are a natural part of the journey towards success. With a can-do attitude, we see setbacks as opportunities to learn and grow, rather than as failures. We must be kind and compassionate to ourselves and remember that every setback is a chance to start again and try a different approach.

In conclusion, developing a can-do attitude is essential for overcoming obstacles and achieving our goals in all areas of life. By identifying and overcoming limiting beliefs, focusing on solutions, persevering, embracing challenges, and taking

33: USING A CAN-DO ATTITUDE TO OVERCOME OBSTACLES AND CHALLENGES

care of our physical and mental health, we can cultivate a positive, proactive mindset that will serve us well in all areas of life. With a can-do attitude, we can unlock our true potential and achieve unprecedented success.

34: The Connection between a Can-Do Attitude and Financial Success

Introduction:

In today's world, financial success is something that almost everyone strives for. Whether it's a luxurious lifestyle or simply financial stability, money is a necessary component of our lives. However, financial success is not something that everyone is able to achieve. Despite hard work and dedication, many people are unable to attain financial prosperity. The reason for this is often tied to their mindset and attitude towards money. In this chapter, we will explore the connection between a can-do attitude and financial success.

What is a Can-Do Attitude?

Before we delve into the connection between a can-do attitude and financial success, let's first define what a can-do attitude is. A can-do attitude is a mindset that is characterized by a positive outlook, resilience, and a willingness to take on challenges. It's an attitude that says "I can do this" rather than "I can't do this." People with a can-do attitude tend to be more proactive and less reactive, they take ownership of their lives, and they are not afraid to take risks.

The Connection between a Can-Do Attitude and Financial
Success:

Now that we understand what a can-do attitude is, let's explore its connection to financial success. People with a can-do attitude tend to be more successful financially than those who have a negative mindset. There are several reasons for this.

People with a Can-Do Attitude are More Likely to Take Risks:

Financial success often requires taking risks. Whether it's starting a business, investing in the stock market, or taking on a new job, there is always a degree of risk involved. People with a can-do attitude are more willing to take risks than those with a negative mindset. They see challenges as opportunities to grow and learn, rather than as obstacles to avoid.

People with a Can-Do Attitude Have a Growth Mindset:

A growth mindset is a belief that one's abilities and intelligence can be developed through hard work, dedication, and perseverance. People with a can-do attitude tend to have a growth mindset, which allows them to see setbacks as opportunities to learn and grow. They are not deterred by failure, but instead use it as a stepping stone to success.

People with a Can-Do Attitude are More Resilient:

Financial success often requires resilience in the face of setbacks and obstacles. People with a can-do attitude tend to be more resilient than those with a negative mindset. They are able to bounce back from failures and setbacks, and are not easily discouraged.

People with a Can-Do Attitude are More Likely to Take Action:

Financial success requires taking action. People with a can-do attitude are more likely to take action than those with a negative mindset. They don't wait for opportunities to come to them, but instead go out and create their own opportunities. They are proactive in pursuing their goals and dreams.

People with a Can-Do Attitude are More Likely to Persist:

34: THE CONNECTION BETWEEN A CAN-DO ATTITUDE AND FINANCIAL SUCCESS

Financial success often requires persistence in the face of obstacles and setbacks. People with a can-do attitude are more likely to persist than those with a negative mindset. They don't give up easily, but instead keep pushing forward towards their goals. They have a strong sense of determination and perseverance.

Conclusion:

In conclusion, there is a strong connection between a can-do attitude and financial success. People with a can-do attitude are more likely to take risks, have a growth mindset, be more resilient, take action, and persist in the face of obstacles. If you want to achieve financial success, it's important to cultivate a can-do attitude. This can be done through self-reflection, positive self-talk, and surrounding yourself with positive influences. By adopting a can-do attitude, you can unlock your true potential and achieve unprecedented success in all areas of your life, including financial success. However, it's important to note that a can-do attitude alone is not enough to guarantee financial success. It's important to also have financial knowledge, discipline, and a solid plan. A can-do attitude can help you overcome obstacles and setbacks along the way, but it's important to also have a clear direction and strategy.

One way to develop a can-do attitude towards finances is to shift your mindset from scarcity to abundance. Scarcity mindset is the belief that there is a limited amount of resources available, and therefore, we must be competitive and guard our resources closely. Abundance mindset, on the other hand, is the belief that there is an unlimited amount of resources available, and we can create opportunities for ourselves and others. By adopting an abundance mindset, we become more open to opportunities and more willing to take risks.

Another way to develop a can-do attitude towards finances is to focus on your strengths and talents. Instead of focusing on your weaknesses and limitations, focus on what you can do and what you're good at. This will give you more confidence in pursuing financial success and help you identify opportunities that align with your strengths.

It's also important to surround yourself with positive influences. Surround yourself with people who have a can-do attitude towards life and finances. This will help you stay motivated and inspired to pursue financial success. Additionally, seek out mentors and coaches who can provide guidance and support in your financial journey.

Finally, it's important to celebrate your successes along the way. Financial success is a journey, and it's important to acknowledge and celebrate your achievements along the way. This will help you stay motivated and inspired to continue pursuing financial success.

In conclusion, a can-do attitude is a powerful tool for achieving financial success. By adopting a positive mindset, taking risks, having a growth mindset, being resilient, taking action, and persisting in the face of obstacles, you can unlock your true potential and achieve unprecedented success in all areas of your life, including financial success. However, it's important to remember that a can-do attitude alone is not enough. It's important to also have financial knowledge, discipline, and a solid plan. By combining a can-do attitude with financial knowledge and discipline, you can achieve the financial success you desire.

35: Using a Can-Do Attitude to Make a Positive Impact on the World

The power of a can-do attitude is immense. It can help you achieve success in all areas of life, from personal to professional. But it can also have a much wider impact. With a can-do attitude, you can make a positive impact on the world around you.

In this chapter, we will explore how you can use a can-do attitude to make a difference in the world. We will look at some examples of people who have done this, and we will provide you with some practical tips on how you can do the same.

The first step in making a positive impact on the world is to believe that you can. A can-do attitude is all about believing that anything is possible if you put your mind to it. If you believe that you can make a difference, then you will be much more likely to take action and make it happen.

One of the most inspiring examples of someone who used a can-do attitude to make a positive impact on the world is Mahatma Gandhi. Gandhi believed that he could use nonviolent resistance to bring about change in India, and he was right. Through his leadership, India gained its independence from British rule, and he inspired countless others around the world to fight for freedom and justice.

Another example is Malala Yousafzai. Malala is an advocate for girls' education and has been a powerful voice for change in Pakistan and around the world. She was shot by the Taliban in 2012, but she refused to be silenced. She continued to speak out, and she became the youngest-ever Nobel Peace Prize laureate in 2014.

These are just two examples of people who used a can-do attitude to make a positive impact on the world. But you don't have to be a famous leader to make a difference. You can start right where you are, with the resources and skills you have right now.

So, how can you use a can-do attitude to make a positive impact on the world? Here are some practical tips:

Identify the issues that matter to you.

The first step is to identify the issues that matter to you.

35: USING A CAN-DO ATTITUDE TO MAKE A POSITIVE IMPACT ON THE WORLD

What are the causes that you are passionate about? What are the issues that you want to see change in? Once you have identified these issues, you can start to think about how you can make a difference.

Educate yourself.

The next step is to educate yourself about the issues that matter to you. Read books, watch documentaries, and talk to people who are involved in these issues. The more you know, the better equipped you will be to make a difference.

Take action.

The most important step is to take action. You can start small by volunteering your time or donating money to organizations that are working to address the issues you care about. You can also start to think about how you can use your skills and resources to make a difference.

Be persistent.

Making a positive impact on the world is not easy, and it often requires persistence and resilience. There will be setbacks and obstacles along the way, but a can-do attitude means that you don't give up. You keep pushing forward, even when things get tough.

Inspire others.

Finally, a can-do attitude is contagious. When you take action and make a positive impact on the world, you inspire others to do the same. Share your story, talk about your experiences, and encourage others to get involved.

In conclusion, using a can-do attitude to make a positive impact on the world is not just possible, it's essential. We all have the power to make a difference, and it starts with believing that we can. Identify the issues that matter to you, educate yourself, take action, be persistent, and inspire others. With these steps, you can make a positive impact on the world and leave a lasting legacy for future generations.

But it's important to remember that making a positive impact doesn't always have to involve grand gestures or monumental achievements. Small acts of kindness, compassion, and generosity can have a ripple effect and create positive change in the world.

35: USING A CAN-DO ATTITUDE TO MAKE A POSITIVE IMPACT ON THE WORLD

For example, volunteering at a local shelter, donating to a charity, or simply showing kindness to a stranger can make a huge difference in someone's life. These actions may seem small, but they can have a big impact on the world around us.

In addition to making a positive impact on the world, having a can-do attitude can also have a positive impact on our own lives. When we believe in ourselves and our abilities, we are more likely to take risks, pursue our passions, and achieve our goals.

A can-do attitude also helps us to overcome obstacles and challenges that we may encounter along the way. Instead of giving up when faced with adversity, we approach problems with a positive mindset and a willingness to find solutions.

This resilience and determination not only helps us to achieve our own goals but also inspires others to do the same. When we lead by example and show others what is possible with a can-do attitude, we create a culture of positivity and growth that benefits everyone around us.

In conclusion, a can-do attitude is a powerful tool that can help us make a positive impact on the world and achieve our own personal goals. It all starts with believing in ourselves and our abilities, and taking action to create positive change. So let's embrace the power of a can-do attitude and work together to make the world a better place for all.

36: Conclusion: Embrace Your Can-Do Attitude and Achieve Unprecedented Success

Congratulations! You've made it through the entire book and reached the conclusion. By now, you should have a better understanding of what a can-do attitude is and how it can help you achieve unprecedented success in all areas of life.

Throughout the book, we've discussed various topics such as the importance of mindset, how to overcome limiting beliefs, and how to cultivate the mindset of winners. We've also talked about the power of positive thinking, visualization, and goal setting.

Now, it's time to put all of these concepts into practice and start embracing your can-do attitude. Remember, a can-do attitude is all about believing in yourself and your ability to achieve your goals. It's about staying positive even when things get tough and finding ways to overcome obstacles.

The first step to embracing your can-do attitude is to identify your limiting beliefs. What is holding you back from achieving your goals? Is it fear of failure? Lack of confidence? Once you've identified your limiting beliefs, you can start working on overcoming them.

One way to overcome limiting beliefs is to practice positive self-talk. Instead of telling yourself that you can't do something, tell yourself that you can. For example, instead of saying "I can't lose weight," say "I am capable of losing weight, and I will do what it takes to achieve my goal."

Visualization is another powerful tool that can help you embrace your can-do attitude. Visualize yourself achieving your goals and imagine how it will feel once you've accomplished them. This will help you stay motivated and focused on your goals.

Goal setting is also essential to cultivating a can-do attitude. Set realistic goals that are challenging but achievable. Break them down into smaller, manageable tasks, and create a plan of action to achieve them.

Finally, surround yourself with positive, supportive people who believe in you and your ability to achieve your goals. Avoid negative people who bring you down and make it harder for you to stay motivated.

36: CONCLUSION: EMBRACE YOUR CAN-DO ATTITUDE AND ACHIEVE UNPRECEDENTED SUCCESS

In conclusion, a can-do attitude is a powerful tool that can help you achieve unprecedented success in all areas of life. It's about believing in yourself and your ability to achieve your goals, staying positive even when things get tough, and finding ways to overcome obstacles. By embracing your can-do attitude and putting the concepts discussed in this book into practice, you can unlock your true potential and achieve the success you've always dreamed of.

Thank You

As we reach the end of this book, I want to say thanks for reading this book.

I want to get this information out to as many people as possible. If you found this book helpful, I would greatly appreciate you leaving me a review. This helps others find the book as well.

Disclaimer

This document is geared towards providing exact and reliable information in regards to the topic and issue covered. The publication is sold on the idea that the publisher is not required to render an accounting, officially permitted, or otherwise, qualified services. If advice is necessary, legal, financial, medical or professional, a practiced individual in the profession should be ordered.

This information is not presented by a financial or medical practitioner and is for entertainment, educational and informational purposes only. The content is not intended as a substitute for professional medical advice, diagnosis, or treatment. Always seek the advice of your physician or other qualified health care provider with any questions you may have regarding a medical condition. Never disregard professional medical advice or delay in seeking it because of something you have read.

The information provided herein is stated to be truthful and consistent, in that any liability, in terms of inattention or otherwise, by any usage or abuse of any policies, processes, or directions contained within is the solitary and utter responsibility of the recipient reader. Under no circumstances

DISCLAIMER

will any legal responsibility or blame be held against the publisher for any reparation, damages, or monetary loss due to the information herein, either directly or indirectly.

www.ingramcontent.com/pod-product-compliance
Lightning Source LLC
Chambersburg PA
CBHW060507130626
46553CB00002B/429